1,001
BIBLE
PROMISES

for a

Powerful

Faith

Compiled by Linda Hang.

Print ISBN 978-1-63609-073-3

Published by Barbour Publishing, Inc., 1810 Barbour Drive, Uhrichsville, Ohio 44683, www.barbourbooks.com

Our mission is to inspire the world with the life-changing message of the Bible.

Member of the
Evangelical Christian
Publishers Association

Printed in the United States of America.

1,001
BIBLE
PROMISES
for a
Powerful
Faith

BARBOUR
PUBLISHING

INTRODUCTION

It's often easy to get weighed down with the disappointments and challenges of life. Without realizing it, our hearts become heavy and our hope for a fulfilling life turns sour.

In His kindness, God has provided uplifting promises of help and encouragement for His children within the pages of His Word, the Bible. Whatever our needs, we can find in scripture the principles we need to address the issues we face.

This collection of 1,001 of scripture's most encouraging promises is the perfect everyday pick-me-up. This book is not intended to replace regular, personal Bible study. It is, however, a quick guide to hundreds of the most uplifting scriptures in the Bible. We hope it will be an encouragement to you as you read.

1

*The LORD is nigh unto them that are of a broken heart;
and saveth such as be of a contrite spirit.*

PSALM 34:18

2

*There remaineth therefore a rest to the people of God.
For he that is entered into his rest, he also hath ceased
from his own works, as God did from his.*

HEBREWS 4:9–10

3

*The bows of the mighty men are broken, and they
that stumbled are girded with strength.*

1 SAMUEL 2:4

4

*And they rose early in the morning, and went forth into the
wilderness of Tekoa: and as they went forth, Jehoshaphat
stood and said, Hear me, O Judah, and ye inhabitants of
Jerusalem; Believe in the LORD your God, so shall ye be
established; believe his prophets, so shall ye prosper.*

2 CHRONICLES 20:20

5

*In the beginning was the Word, and the Word
was with God, and the Word was God.*

JOHN 1:1

6

*And blessed is she that believed: for there
shall be a performance of those things
which were told her from the Lord.*

LUKE 1:45

7

*For I am not ashamed of the gospel of Christ: for it is
the power of God unto salvation to every one that
believeth; to the Jew first, and also to the Greek.*
ROMANS 1:16

8

*As ye have therefore received Christ Jesus the Lord, so walk ye
in him: rooted and built up in him, and stablished in the faith,
as ye have been taught, abounding therein with thanksgiving.*
COLOSSIANS 2:6–7

9

*I am crucified with Christ: nevertheless I live; yet not I,
but Christ liveth in me: and the life which I now live
in the flesh I live by the faith of the Son of God,
who loved me, and gave himself for me.*
GALATIANS 2:20

10

*Only take heed to thyself, and keep thy soul diligently, lest
thou forget the things which thine eyes have seen, and lest
they depart from thy heart all the days of thy life: but teach
them thy sons, and thy sons' sons; specially the day that thou
stoodest before the LORD thy God in Horeb, when the Lord
said unto me, Gather me the people together, and I will
make them hear my words, that they may learn to fear
me all the days that they shall live upon the earth,
and that they may teach their children.*
DEUTERONOMY 4:9–10

11

*But the meek shall inherit the earth; and shall
delight themselves in the abundance of peace.*
PSALM 37:11

12

*I acknowledge my sin unto thee, and mine iniquity have
I not hid. I said, I will confess my transgressions unto the
LORD; and thou forgavest the iniquity of my sin.*
PSALM 32:5

13

*But whoso hearkeneth unto me shall dwell safely,
and shall be quiet from fear of evil.*
PROVERBS 1:33

14

*For I am the LORD, I change not;
therefore ye sons of Jacob are not consumed.*
MALACHI 3:6

15

*The LORD God is my strength, and he will make my feet
like hinds' feet, and he will make me to walk upon mine
high places. To the chief singer on my stringed instruments.*
HABAKKUK 3:19

16

*If then God so clothe the grass, which is to day in the field,
and to morrow is cast into the oven; how much more
will he clothe you, O ye of little faith?*
LUKE 12:28

17

And will be a Father unto you, and ye shall be my sons and daughters, saith the Lord Almighty.
2 CORINTHIANS 6:18

18

He that descended is the same also that ascended up far above all heavens, that he might fill all things.
EPHESIANS 4:10

19

Wherefore also it is contained in the scripture, Behold, I lay in Sion a chief corner stone, elect, precious: and he that believeth on him shall not be confounded.
1 PETER 2:6

20

For the Lord taketh pleasure in his people: he will beautify the meek with salvation.
PSALM 149:4

21

The soul of the sluggard desireth, and hath nothing: but the soul of the diligent shall be made fat.
PROVERBS 13:4

22

And, behold, I am with thee, and will keep thee in all places whither thou goest, and will bring thee again into this land; for I will not leave thee, until I have done that which I have spoken to thee of.
GENESIS 28:15

23

*In whom we have redemption through his blood, the
forgiveness of sins, according to the riches of his grace.*
EPHESIANS 1:7

24

*If my people, which are called by my name, shall humble
themselves, and pray, and seek my face, and turn from
their wicked ways; then will I hear from heaven,
and will forgive their sin, and will heal their land.*
2 CHRONICLES 7:14

25

*In the way of righteousness is life: and in
the pathway thereof there is no death.*
PROVERBS 12:28

26

*Remembering mine affliction and my misery, the
wormwood and the gall. . . . This I recall to my mind,
therefore have I hope. It is of the LORD's mercies that we
are not consumed, because his compassions fail not.*
LAMENTATIONS 3:19, 21–22

27

*And I will bring the third part through the fire, and will
refine them as silver is refined, and will try them as gold is
tried: they shall call on my name, and I will hear them: I will
say, It is my people: and they shall say, The LORD is my God.*
ZECHARIAH 13:9

28

For God so loved the world, that he gave his only begotten Son, that whosoever believeth in him should not perish, but have everlasting life.

John 3:16

29

For the promise is unto you, and to your children, and to all that are afar off, even as many as the LORD our God shall call.

Acts 2:39

30

Whom I have sent unto you for the same purpose, that he might know your estate, and comfort your hearts.

Colossians 4:8

31

The LORD is longsuffering, and of great mercy, forgiving iniquity and transgression, and by no means clearing the guilty, visiting the iniquity of the fathers upon the children unto the third and fourth generation.

Numbers 14:18

32

There shall not any man be able to stand before thee all the days of thy life: as I was with Moses, so I will be with thee: I will not fail thee, nor forsake thee.

Joshua 1:5

33

But when we are judged, we are chastened of the Lord, that we should not be condemned with the world.

1 Corinthians 11:32

34

*By this I know that thou favourest me, because mine enemy
doth not triumph over me. And as for me, thou upholdest
me in mine integrity, and settest me before thy face for ever.*
PSALM 41:11–12

35

*The LORD thy God in the midst of thee is mighty; he will
save, he will rejoice over thee with joy; he will rest in
his love, he will joy over thee with singing.*
ZEPHANIAH 3:17

36

*And ye shall be betrayed both by parents, and brethren,
and kinsfolks, and friends; and some of you shall they cause
to be put to death. And ye shall be hated of all men for my
name's sake. But there shall not an hair of your head
perish. In your patience possess ye your souls.*
LUKE 21:16–19

37

*He hath shewed thee, O man, what is good; and what
doth the LORD require of thee, but to do justly, and to
love mercy, and to walk humbly with thy God?*
MICAH 6:8

38

*For the hope which is laid up for you in heaven, whereof
ye heard before in the word of the truth of the gospel.*
COLOSSIANS 1:5

39

*He that hath an ear, let him hear what the Spirit
saith unto the churches; He that overcometh
shall not be hurt of the second death.*

REVELATION 2:11

40

*Whosoever transgresseth, and abideth not in the doctrine
of Christ, hath not God. He that abideth in the doctrine
of Christ, he hath both the Father and the Son.*

2 JOHN 1:9

41

*And thou shalt shew thy son in that day, saying,
This is done because of that which the LORD did
unto me when I came forth out of Egypt.*

EXODUS 13:8

42

*I sought the LORD, and he heard me,
and delivered me from all my fears.*

PSALM 34:4

43

*Honour the Lord with thy substance, and with the
firstfruits of all thine increase: so shall thy barns be filled
with plenty, and thy presses shall burst out with new wine.*

PROVERBS 3:9–10

44

*Unto the upright there ariseth light in the darkness:
he is gracious, and full of compassion, and righteous.*

PSALM 112:4

45

*Humble yourselves therefore under the mighty
hand of God, that he may exalt you in due time.*
1 PETER 5:6

46

*Return unto thy rest, O my soul; for the
Lord hath dealt bountifully with thee.*
PSALM 116:7

47

*And saying, The time is fulfilled, and the kingdom of
God is at hand: repent ye, and believe the gospel.*
MARK 1:15

48

*Not that we are sufficient of ourselves to think any
thing as of ourselves; but our sufficiency is of God.*
2 CORINTHIANS 3:5

49

*I press toward the mark for the prize of
the high calling of God in Christ Jesus.*
PHILIPPIANS 3:14

50

*How that they told you there should be mockers in the
last time, who should walk after their own ungodly lusts.
These be they who separate themselves, sensual, having not
the Spirit. But ye, beloved, building up yourselves on your
most holy faith, praying in the Holy Ghost, keep yourselves
in the love of God, looking for the mercy of our
Lord Jesus Christ unto eternal life.*
JUDE 18–21

51

*This book of the law shall not depart out of thy mouth;
but thou shalt meditate therein day and night, that thou
mayest observe to do according to all that is written
therein: for then thou shalt make thy way prosperous,
and then thou shalt have good success.*

Joshua 1:8

52

*For I was ashamed to require of the king a band of soldiers
and horsemen to help us against the enemy in the way:
because we had spoken unto the king, saying, The hand of
our God is upon all them for good that seek him; but his
power and his wrath is against all them that forsake him.*

Ezra 8:22

53

Know therefore that the LORD *thy God, he is God,
the faithful God, which keepeth covenant and mercy
with them that love him and keep his commandments
to a thousand generations.*

Deuteronomy 7:9

54

*Blessed is the man that walketh not in the counsel of the
ungodly, nor standeth in the way of sinners, nor sitteth in
the seat of the scornful. But his delight is in the law of the*
LORD; *and in his law doth he meditate day and night.*

Psalm 1:1–2

55

I acknowledge my sin unto thee, and mine iniquity have I not hid. I said, I will confess my transgressions unto the LORD; and thou forgavest the iniquity of my sin.
PSALM 32:5

56

O Lord, thou art my God; I will exalt thee, I will praise thy name; for thou hast done wonderful things; thy counsels of old are faithfulness and truth.
ISAIAH 25:1

57

He will regard the prayer of the destitute, and not despise their prayer.
PSALM 102:17

58

If it be so, our God whom we serve is able to deliver us from the burning fiery furnace, and he will deliver us out of thine hand, O king.
DANIEL 3:17

59

The LORD openeth the eyes of the blind: the LORD raiseth them that are bowed down: the LORD loveth the righteous.
PSALM 146:8

60

Heaviness in the heart of man maketh it stoop:
but a good word maketh it glad.

PROVERBS 12:25

61

For he shall give his angels charge over thee, to keep
thee in all thy ways. They shall bear thee up in their
hands, lest thou dash thy foot against a stone.

PSALM 91:11–12

62

Blessed are they that keep judgment, and he
that doeth righteousness at all times.

PSALM 106:3

63

And I will sow her unto me in the earth; and I will have
mercy upon her that had not obtained mercy; and I will
say to them which were not my people, Thou art my
people; and they shall say, Thou art my God.

HOSEA 2:23

64

For there is nothing hid, which shall not be
manifested; neither was any thing kept secret,
but that it should come abroad.

MARK 4:22

65

For the kingdom of God is not in word, but in power.
1 Corinthians 4:20

66

*For the Lord himself shall descend from heaven with a shout,
with the voice of the archangel, and with the trump of God:
and the dead in Christ shall rise first: then we which are alive
and remain shall be caught up together with them in the clouds,
to meet the Lord in the air: and so shall we ever be with the
Lord. Wherefore comfort one another with these words.*
1 Thessalonians 4:16–18

67

*Blessed is the man that endureth temptation: for when
he is tried, he shall receive the crown of life, which the
Lord hath promised to them that love him.*
James 1:12

68

*For when God made promise to Abraham, because he
could swear by no greater, he sware by himself, saying,
Surely blessing I will bless thee, and multiplying
I will multiply thee. And so, after he had patiently
endured, he obtained the promise.*
Hebrews 6:13–15

69

*Then he said unto them, Go your way, eat the fat, and
drink the sweet, and send portions unto them for whom
nothing is prepared: for this day is holy unto our Lord:
neither be ye sorry; for the joy of the Lord is your strength.*

Nehemiah 8:10

70

*Many are the afflictions of the righteous:
but the Lord delivereth him out of them all.*

Psalm 34:19

71

*Blessed are the poor in spirit:
for theirs is the kingdom of heaven.*

Matthew 5:3

72

*That the trial of your faith, being much more precious
than of gold that perisheth, though it be tried with fire,
might be found unto praise and honour and
glory at the appearing of Jesus Christ.*

1 Peter 1:7

73

And the LORD passed by before him, and proclaimed,
The LORD, The LORD God, merciful and gracious,
longsuffering, and abundant in goodness and truth.
EXODUS 34:6

74

I am sought of them that asked not for me; I am found of
them that sought me not: I said, Behold me, behold me.
ISAIAH 65:1

75

Thy congregation hath dwelt therein: thou, O God,
hast prepared of thy goodness for the poor.
PSALM 68:10

76

For the vision is yet for an appointed time, but at the end
it shall speak, and not lie: though it tarry, wait for it;
because it will surely come, it will not tarry.
HABAKKUK 2:3

77

Draw nigh to God, and he will draw nigh to you.
Cleanse your hands, ye sinners; and purify
your hearts, ye double minded.
JAMES 4:8

78

My little children, these things write I unto you, that
ye sin not. And if any man sin, we have an advocate
with the Father, Jesus Christ the righteous: and he is
the propitiation for our sins: and not for ours only,
but also for the sins of the whole world.

1 John 2:1–2

79

And the Lord said unto him, Peace be
unto thee; fear not: thou shalt not die.

Judges 6:23

80

And thou shalt be secure, because there is hope; yea, thou
shalt dig about thee, and thou shalt take thy rest in safety.
Also thou shalt lie down, and none shall make thee
afraid; yea, many shall make suit unto thee.

Job 11:18–19

81

For God is my King of old, working salvation
in the midst of the earth.

Psalm 74:12

82

Also unto thee, O Lord, belongeth mercy: for thou
renderest to every man according to his work.

Psalm 62:12

83

Whosoever abideth in him sinneth not: whosoever
sinneth hath not seen him, neither known him.
1 JOHN 3:6

84

And he that overcometh, and keepeth my works unto
the end, to him will I give power over the nations.
REVELATION 2:26

85

The LORD is my strength and song, and he is become
my salvation: he is my God, and I will prepare him an
habitation; my father's God, and I will exalt him.
EXODUS 15:2

86

For thus saith the LORD unto the house of Israel,
Seek ye me, and ye shall live.
AMOS 5:4

87

I will bear the indignation of the LORD, because I have
sinned against him, until he plead my cause, and execute
judgment for me: he will bring me forth to the light,
and I shall behold his righteousness.
MICAH 7:9

88

Mine eyes fail for thy salvation,
and for the word of thy righteousness.
PSALM 119:123

89

Thus saith the LORD, Stand ye in the ways, and see,
and ask for the old paths, where is the good way,
and walk therein, and ye shall find rest for your souls.
But they said, We will not walk therein.
JEREMIAH 6:16

90

Fools make a mock at sin: but among
the righteous there is favour.
PROVERBS 14:9

91

In the multitude of my thoughts within
me thy comforts delight my soul.
PSALM 94:19

92

A new heart also will I give you, and a new spirit will I
put within you: and I will take away the stony heart out
of your flesh, and I will give you an heart of flesh.
EZEKIEL 36:26

93

Therefore I say unto you, Take no thought for your life, what ye shall eat, or what ye shall drink; nor yet for your body, what ye shall put on. Is not the life more than meat, and the body than raiment?
MATTHEW 6:25

94

For the word of God is quick, and powerful, and sharper than any twoedged sword, piercing even to the dividing asunder of soul and spirit, and of the joints and marrow, and is a discerner of the thoughts and intents of the heart.
HEBREWS 4:12

95

Then when lust hath conceived, it bringeth forth sin: and sin, when it is finished, bringeth forth death.
JAMES 1:15

96

It is vain for you to rise up early, to sit up late, to eat the bread of sorrows: for so he giveth his beloved sleep.
PSALM 127:2

97

And whosoever shall exalt himself shall be abased; and he that shall humble himself shall be exalted.
MATTHEW 23:12

98

Also regard not your stuff; for the good
of all the land of Egypt is your's.

GENESIS 45:20

99

He shall deliver thee in six troubles:
yea, in seven there shall no evil touch thee.

JOB 5:19

100

He will fulfil the desire of them that fear him:
he also will hear their cry, and will save them.

PSALM 145:19

101

To him give all the prophets witness, that through his name
whosoever believeth in him shall receive remission of sins.

ACTS 10:43

102

And Jesus said unto them, I am the bread of life:
he that cometh to me shall never hunger;
and he that believeth on me shall never thirst.

JOHN 6:35

103

If the Son therefore shall make you free,
ye shall be free indeed.
JOHN 8:36

104

Therefore being justified by faith, we have peace
with God through our Lord Jesus Christ.
ROMANS 5:1

105

And I say unto you, Ask, and it shall be given you; seek,
and ye shall find; knock, and it shall be opened unto you.
LUKE 11:9

106

Say ye to the righteous, that it shall be well with him:
for they shall eat the fruit of their doings.
ISAIAH 3:10

107

And he shall be like a tree planted by the rivers of water,
that bringeth forth his fruit in his season; his leaf also
shall not wither; and whatsoever he doeth shall prosper.
The ungodly are not so: but are like the chaff
which the wind driveth away.
PSALM 1:3–4

108

*But I am poor and needy; yet the Lord thinketh
upon me: thou art my help and my deliverer;
make no tarrying, O my God.*

PSALM 40:17

109

*Return, ye backsliding children, and I will heal
your backslidings. Behold, we come unto thee;
for thou art the LORD our God.*

JEREMIAH 3:22

110

*The LORD is good, a strong hold in the day of trouble;
and he knoweth them that trust in him.*

NAHUM 1:7

111

*Because thou hast kept the word of my patience, I also
will keep thee from the hour of temptation, which shall
come upon all the world, to try them that dwell upon
the earth. Behold, I come quickly: hold that fast which
thou hast, that no man take thy crown.*

REVELATION 3:10–11

112

*And the work of righteousness shall be peace; and the effect
of righteousness quietness and assurance for ever.*

ISAIAH 32:17

113

Thou hast turned for me my mourning into dancing: thou hast put off my sackcloth, and girded me with gladness.
PSALM 30:11

114

To set up on high those that be low; that those which mourn may be exalted to safety.
JOB 5:11

115

For whosoever shall do the will of my Father which is in heaven, the same is my brother, and sister, and mother.
MATTHEW 12:50

116

But he giveth more grace.
JAMES 4:6

117

For if these things be in you, and abound, they make you that ye shall neither be barren nor unfruitful in the knowledge of our Lord Jesus Christ.
2 PETER 1:8

118

I will instruct thee and teach thee in the way which thou shalt go: I will guide thee with mine eye.
PSALM 32:8

119

For whosoever will save his life shall lose it;
but whosoever shall lose his life for my sake
and the gospel's, the same shall save it.

MARK 8:35

120

And hope maketh not ashamed; because the love of
God is shed abroad in our hearts by the Holy
Ghost which is given unto us.

ROMANS 5:5

121

Be not deceived; God is not mocked: for whatsoever
a man soweth, that shall he also reap.

GALATIANS 6:7

122

There hath no temptation taken you but such as is
common to man: but God is faithful, who will not
suffer you to be tempted above that ye are able;
but will with the temptation also make a way
to escape, that ye may be able to bear it.

1 CORINTHIANS 10:13

123

I will both lay me down in peace, and sleep:
for thou, LORD, only makest me dwell in safety.

PSALM 4:8

124

The wicked is driven away in his wickedness:
but the righteous hath hope in his death.

PROVERBS 14:32

125

*And the Lord said unto Moses, Is the Lord's hand
waxed short? thou shalt see now whether my
word shall come to pass unto thee or not.*
Numbers 11:23

126

*Be patient therefore, brethren, unto the coming of the Lord.
Behold, the husbandman waiteth for the precious fruit of
the earth, and hath long patience for it, until he receive
the early and latter rain. Be ye also patient; stablish your
hearts: for the coming of the Lord draweth nigh.*
James 5:7–8

127

*Beloved, if our heart condemn us not,
then have we confidence toward God.*
1 John 3:21

128

But godliness with contentment is great gain.
1 Timothy 6:6

129

*But after that the kindness and love of God our Saviour
toward man appeared, not by works of righteousness which
we have done, but according to his mercy he saved us, by the
washing of regeneration, and renewing of the Holy Ghost.*
Titus 3:4–5

130

*And being made perfect, he became the author of
eternal salvation unto all them that obey him.*
Hebrews 5:9

131

*The Lord knoweth how to deliver the godly out
of temptations, and to reserve the unjust unto
the day of judgment to be punished.*

2 PETER 2:9

132

*But love ye your enemies, and do good, and lend,
hoping for nothing again; and your reward shall be great,
and ye shall be the children of the Highest: for he is
kind unto the unthankful and to the evil.*

LUKE 6:35

133

*Verily, verily, I say unto you, He that heareth my word,
and believeth on him that sent me, hath everlasting
life, and shall not come into condemnation;
but is passed from death unto life.*

JOHN 5:24

134

*Then Jesus beholding him loved him, and said unto him,
One thing thou lackest: go thy way, sell whatsoever thou
hast, and give to the poor, and thou shalt have treasure in
heaven: and come, take up the cross, and follow me.*

MARK 10:21

135

*For God giveth to a man that is good in his sight wisdom,
and knowledge, and joy: but to the sinner he giveth travail,
to gather and to heap up, that he may give to him that is
good before God. This also is vanity and vexation of spirit.*

ECCLESIASTES 2:26

136

And therefore will the LORD wait, that he may be gracious unto you, and therefore will he be exalted, that he may have mercy upon you: for the LORD is a God of judgment: blessed are all they that wait for him.

ISAIAH 30:18

137

Sing unto the LORD, praise ye the LORD: for he hath delivered the soul of the poor from the hand of evildoers.

JEREMIAH 20:13

138

Be merciful unto me, O God, be merciful unto me: for my soul trusteth in thee: yea, in the shadow of thy wings will I make my refuge, until these calamities be overpast.

PSALM 57:1

139

Be thou my strong habitation, whereunto I may continually resort: thou hast given commandment to save me; for thou art my rock and my fortress.

PSALM 71:3

140

Although my house be not so with God; yet he hath made with me an everlasting covenant, ordered in all things, and sure: for this is all my salvation, and all my desire, although he make it not to grow.

2 SAMUEL 23:5

141

But the hour cometh, and now is, when the true worshippers shall worship the Father in spirit and in truth: for the Father seeketh such to worship him.

JOHN 4:23

142

Repent ye therefore, and be converted, that your sins may be blotted out, when the times of refreshing shall come from the presence of the Lord.

ACTS 3:19

143

Blessed is every one that feareth the LORD; that walketh in his ways.

PSALM 128:1

144

Thou shalt be hid from the scourge of the tongue: neither shalt thou be afraid of destruction when it cometh.

JOB 5:21

145

The LORD is good unto them that wait for him, to the soul that seeketh him.

LAMENTATIONS 3:25

146

Bring ye all the tithes into the storehouse, that there may be meat in mine house, and prove me now herewith, saith the LORD of hosts, if I will not open you the windows of heaven, and pour you out a blessing, that there shall not be room enough to receive it.

MALACHI 3:10

147

For thou, Lord, art good, and ready to forgive;
and plenteous in mercy unto all them that call upon thee.
PSALM 86:5

148

And they shall no more be a prey to the heathen, neither
shall the beast of the land devour them; but they shall
dwell safely, and none shall make them afraid.
EZEKIEL 34:28

149

I have shewed you all things, how that so labouring ye ought
to support the weak, and to remember the words of the Lord
Jesus, how he said, It is more blessed to give than to receive.
ACTS 20:35

150

He that loveth his brother abideth in the light,
and there is none occasion of stumbling in him.
I JOHN 2:10

151

But continue thou in the things which thou
hast learned and hast been assured of,
knowing of whom thou hast learned them.
2 TIMOTHY 3:14

152

That being justified by his grace, we should be made
heirs according to the hope of eternal life.
TITUS 3:7

153

The LORD is gracious, and full of compassion;
slow to anger, and of great mercy.
PSALM 145:8

154

Fear thou not; for I am with thee: be not dismayed; for I am
thy God: I will strengthen thee; yea, I will help thee; yea,
I will uphold thee with the right hand of my righteousness.
ISAIAH 41:10

155

Like as a father pitieth his children,
so the LORD pitieth them that fear him.
PSALM 103:13

156

That we should be saved from our enemies, and from the
hand of all that hate us; to perform the mercy promised
to our fathers, and to remember his holy covenant.
LUKE 1:71–72

157

For thou, LORD, wilt bless the righteous; with favour
wilt thou compass him as with a shield.
PSALM 5:12

158

For if, when we were enemies, we were reconciled to
God by the death of his Son, much more, being reconciled,
we shall be saved by his life. And not only so, but we also
joy in God through our Lord Jesus Christ, by whom
we have now received the atonement.
ROMANS 5:10–11

159

He shall redeem their soul from deceit and violence:
and precious shall their blood be in his sight.

PSALM 72:14

160

Through God we shall do valiantly: for he
it is that shall tread down our enemies.

PSALM 60:12

161

Nevertheless he left not himself without witness, in that
he did good, and gave us rain from heaven, and fruitful
seasons, filling our hearts with food and gladness.

ACTS 14:17

162

Take heed therefore how ye hear: for whosoever hath,
to him shall be given; and whosoever hath not, from him
shall be taken even that which he seemeth to have.

LUKE 8:18

163

Therefore it is of faith, that it might be by grace; to the end
the promise might be sure to all the seed; not to that only
which is of the law, but to that also which is of the faith
of Abraham; who is the father of us all.

ROMANS 4:16

164

Blessed be God, even the Father of our Lord Jesus Christ,
the Father of mercies, and the God of all comfort;
who comforteth us in all our tribulation, that we may
be able to comfort them which are in any trouble, by the
comfort wherewith we ourselves are comforted of God.
2 Corinthians 1:3–4

165

Wherefore, my beloved, as ye have always obeyed, not as in
my presence only, but now much more in my absence,
work out your own salvation with fear and trembling.
For it is God which worketh in you both to will
and to do of his good pleasure.
Philippians 2:12–13

166

And ye shall serve the Lord your God, and he shall
bless thy bread, and thy water; and I will
take sickness away from the midst of thee.
Exodus 23:25

167

If thou wouldest seek unto God betimes, and make thy
supplication to the Almighty; if thou wert pure and
upright; surely now he would awake for thee, and make
the habitation of thy righteousness prosperous.
Job 8:5–6

168

The Lord is righteous in all his ways,
and holy in all his works.
Psalm 145:17

169

The LORD is merciful and gracious, slow to anger,
and plenteous in mercy.
PSALM 103:8

170

Behold, it is written before me: I will not keep silence,
but will recompense, even recompense into their bosom.
ISAIAH 65:6

171

Light is sown for the righteous, and gladness for the
upright in heart. Rejoice in the Lord, ye righteous;
and give thanks at the remembrance of his holiness.
PSALM 97:11–12

172

And many of them that sleep in the dust of the earth
shall awake, some to everlasting life, and some
to shame and everlasting contempt.
DANIEL 12:2

173

No man hath seen God at any time. If we love one another,
God dwelleth in us, and his love is perfected in us.
1 JOHN 4:12

174

For the which cause I also suffer these things: nevertheless
I am not ashamed: for I know whom I have believed,
and am persuaded that he is able to keep that which
I have committed unto him against that day.
2 TIMOTHY 1:12

175

But the wisdom that is from above is first pure,
then peaceable, gentle, and easy to be intreated,
full of mercy and good fruits, without partiality,
and without hypocrisy.

JAMES 3:17

176

He will swallow up death in victory; and the Lord God
will wipe away tears from off all faces; and the rebuke of
his people shall he take away from off all the earth:
for the Lord hath spoken it.

ISAIAH 25:8

177

The righteousness of the perfect shall direct his way:
but the wicked shall fall by his own wickedness.

PROVERBS 11:5

178

Nevertheless we, according to his promise, look for new
heavens and a new earth, wherein dwelleth righteousness.

2 PETER 3:13

179

Then shall we know, if we follow on to know the LORD: his
going forth is prepared as the morning; and he shall come unto
us as the rain, as the latter and former rain unto the earth.

HOSEA 6:3

180

*Then shall he give the rain of thy seed, that thou shalt sow
the ground withal; and bread of the increase of the earth,
and it shall be fat and plenteous: in that day shall
thy cattle feed in large pastures.*

ISAIAH 30:23

181

And, lo, I am with you always, even unto the end of the world.

MATTHEW 28:20

182

*For the people shall dwell in Zion at Jerusalem: thou shalt
weep no more: he will be very gracious unto thee at the
voice of thy cry; when he shall hear it, he will answer thee.*

ISAIAH 30:19

183

*Lo, children are an heritage of the LORD: and the fruit of
the womb is his reward. As arrows are in the hand of a
mighty man; so are children of the youth. Happy is the man
that hath his quiver full of them: they shall not be ashamed,
but they shall speak with the enemies in the gate.*

PSALM 127:3–5

184

*But as many as received him, to them gave he power to become
the sons of God, even to them that believe on his name.*

JOHN 1:12

185

And he said unto Jesus, Lord, remember me when thou
comest into thy kingdom. And Jesus said unto him, Verily
I say unto thee, Today shalt thou be with me in paradise.

LUKE 23:42–43

186

And he said, My presence shall go with thee,
and I will give thee rest.

EXODUS 33:14

187

For if ye turn again unto the LORD, your brethren and
your children shall find compassion before them that lead
them captive, so that they shall come again into this land:
for the LORD your God is gracious and merciful, and will
not turn away his face from you, if ye return unto him.

2 CHRONICLES 30:9

188

For his anger endureth but a moment; in his
favour is life: weeping may endure for a night,
but joy cometh in the morning.

PSALM 30:5

189

Turn you at my reproof: behold, I will pour out my spirit
unto you, I will make known my words unto you.

PROVERBS 1:23

190

If ye then, being evil, know how to give good gifts unto
your children, how much more shall your Father which
is in heaven give good things to them that ask him?

MATTHEW 7:11

191

Heaven and earth shall pass away,
but my words shall not pass away.
MATTHEW 24:35

192

He staggered not at the promise of God through unbelief;
but was strong in faith, giving glory to God; and being
fully persuaded that, what he had promised,
he was able also to perform.
ROMANS 4:20–21

193

Who being the brightness of his glory, and the express
image of his person, and upholding all things by the word
of his power, when he had by himself purged our sins,
sat down on the right hand of the Majesty on high.
HEBREWS 1:3

194

Thou tellest my wanderings: put thou my tears into thy
bottle: are they not in thy book? When I cry unto thee,
then shall mine enemies turn back: this I know; for God
is for me. In God will I praise his word: in the LORD
will I praise his word. In God have I put my trust:
I will not be afraid what man can do unto me.
PSALM 56:8–11

195

Trust ye in the LORD for ever:
for in the Lord Jehovah is everlasting strength.
ISAIAH 26:4

196

Heal me, O LORD, and I shall be healed; save me,
and I shall be saved: for thou art my praise.

JEREMIAH 17:14

197

And the Spirit and the bride say, Come. And let him that
heareth say, Come. And let him that is athirst come.
And whosoever will, let him take the water of life freely.

REVELATION 22:17

198

A wise man will hear, and will increase learning; and a
man of understanding shall attain unto wise counsels.

PROVERBS 1:5

199

Blessed is the man whom thou chastenest,
O LORD, and teachest him out of thy law;
that thou mayest give him rest from the days
of adversity, until the pit be digged for the wicked.

PSALM 94:12–13

200

But thou, O LORD, art a shield for me; my glory,
and the lifter up of mine head.

PSALM 3:3

201

For all those things hath mine hand made, and all those
things have been, saith the LORD: but to this man will I
look, even to him that is poor and of a contrite spirit,
and trembleth at my word.

ISAIAH 66:2

202

Lay not up for yourselves treasures upon earth, where moth
and rust doth corrupt, and where thieves break through
and steal: but lay up for yourselves treasures in heaven,
where neither moth nor rust doth corrupt, and where
thieves do not break through nor steal: for where your
treasure is, there will your heart be also.

MATTHEW 6:19–21

203

But we are bound to give thanks alway to God for you,
brethren beloved of the Lord, because God hath from the
beginning chosen you to salvation through sanctification
of the Spirit and belief of the truth.

2 THESSALONIANS 2:13

204

In hope of eternal life, which God, that cannot lie,
promised before the world began.

TITUS 1:2

205

But with righteousness shall he judge the poor, and reprove
with equity for the meek of the earth: and he shall smite
the earth: with the rod of his mouth, and with the
breath of his lips shall he slay the wicked.

ISAIAH 11:4

206

Blessed are they that mourn: for they shall be comforted.

MATTHEW 5:4

207

*And rend your heart, and not your garments,
and turn unto the Lord your God: for he is
gracious and merciful, slow to anger, and of great
kindness, and repenteth him of the evil.*

Joel 2:13

208

*So when this corruptible shall have put on incorruption,
and this mortal shall have put on immortality, then shall
be brought to pass the saying that is written, Death is
swallowed up in victory. O death, where is thy sting?
O grave, where is thy victory?*

1 Corinthians 15:54–55

209

*Yea, before the day was I am he; and there is none that can
deliver out of my hand: I will work, and who shall let it?*

Isaiah 43:13

210

*O love the Lord, all ye his saints: for the Lord preserveth
the faithful, and plentifully rewardeth the proud doer.*

Psalm 31:23

211

*God is jealous, and the Lord revengeth; the Lord
revengeth, and is furious; the Lord will take vengeance on
his adversaries, and he reserveth wrath for his enemies.*

Nahum 1:2

212

Whosoever therefore shall humble himself as this little child, the same is greatest in the kingdom of heaven.
MATTHEW 18:4

213

But, beloved, be not ignorant of this one thing, that one day is with the Lord as a thousand years, and a thousand years as one day. The Lord is not slack concerning his promise, as some men count slackness; but is longsuffering to us-ward, not willing that any should perish, but that all should come to repentance.
2 PETER 3:8–9

214

And the world passeth away, and the lust thereof: but he that doeth the will of God abideth for ever.
1 JOHN 2:17

215

For the Lord will not cast off for ever: but though he cause grief, yet will he have compassion according to the multitude of his mercies. For he doth not afflict willingly nor grieve the children of men.
LAMENTATIONS 3:31–33

216

Hath walked in my statutes, and hath kept my judgments, to deal truly; he is just, he shall surely live, saith the Lord God.
EZEKIEL 18:9

217

And the LORD, he it is that doth go before thee;
he will be with thee, he will not fail thee, neither
forsake thee: fear not, neither be dismayed.

DEUTERONOMY 31:8

218

Seek good, and not evil, that ye may live: and so the LORD,
the God of hosts, shall be with you, as ye have spoken.

AMOS 5:14

219

Think not that I am come to destroy the law, or the
prophets: I am not come to destroy, but to fulfil. For verily
I say unto you, Till heaven and earth pass, one jot or one
tittle shall in no wise pass from the law, till all be fulfilled.

MATTHEW 5:17–18

220

For the mountains shall depart, and the hills be
removed; but my kindness shall not depart from thee,
neither shall the covenant of my peace be removed,
saith the LORD that hath mercy on thee.

ISAIAH 54:10

221

But one in a certain place testified, saying, What is man,
that thou art mindful of him? or the son of man that thou
visitest him? Thou madest him a little lower than the angels;
thou crownedst him with glory and honour, and didst set
him over the works of thy hands: thou hast put all things in
subjection under his feet. For in that he put all in subjection
under him, he left nothing that is not put under him.
But now we see not yet all things put under him.

HEBREWS 2:6–8

222

As for man, his days are as grass: as a flower of the field, so he flourisheth. For the wind passeth over it, and it is gone; and the place thereof shall know it no more. But the mercy of the Lord is from everlasting to everlasting upon them that fear him, and his righteousness unto children's children.

Psalm 103:15–17

223

Let no man say when he is tempted, I am tempted of God: for God cannot be tempted with evil, neither tempteth he any man.

James 1:13

224

Be ye therefore merciful, as your Father also is merciful. Judge not, and ye shall not be judged: condemn not, and ye shall not be condemned: forgive, and ye shall be forgiven.

Luke 6:36–37

225

And it shall come to pass in the day that the Lord shall give thee rest from thy sorrow, and from thy fear, and from the hard bondage wherein thou wast made to serve.

Isaiah 14:3

226

Yea, if thou criest after knowledge, and liftest up thy voice for understanding; if thou seekest her as silver, and searchest for her as for hid treasures; then shalt thou understand the fear of the Lord, and find the knowledge of God.

Proverbs 2:3–5

227

For to be carnally minded is death;
but to be spiritually minded is life and peace.
ROMANS 8:6

228

For we are his workmanship, created in
Christ Jesus unto good works, which God hath
before ordained that we should walk in them.
EPHESIANS 2:10

229

For the scripture saith, Whosoever believeth
on him shall not be ashamed.
ROMANS 10:11

230

For thou shalt eat the labour of thine hands:
happy shalt thou be, and it shall be well with thee.
PSALM 128:2

231

So shall they fear the name of the LORD from the west,
and his glory from the rising of the sun. When the enemy
shall come in like a flood, the Spirit of the LORD
shall lift up a standard against him.
ISAIAH 59:19

232

But he that doeth truth cometh to the light, that his deeds
may be made manifest, that they are wrought in God.
JOHN 3:21

233

*As it is written, Behold, I lay in Sion a stumblingstone
and rock of offence: and whosoever believeth on
him shall not be ashamed.*

Romans 9:33

234

*Being confident of this very thing, that he
which hath begun a good work in you will
perform it until the day of Jesus Christ.*

Philippians 1:6

235

*I create the fruit of the lips; Peace, peace to him that is far off,
and to him that is near, saith the LORD; and I will heal him.*

Isaiah 57:19

236

*The LORD also will be a refuge for the oppressed,
a refuge in times of trouble.*

Psalm 9:9

237

*Thou, which hast shewed me great and sore troubles,
shalt quicken me again, and shalt bring me up again
from the depths of the earth. Thou shalt increase
my greatness, and comfort me on every side.*

Psalm 71:20–21

238

*Now if the fall of them be the riches of the world,
and the diminishing of them the riches of the Gentiles;
how much more their fulness?*

Romans 11:12

239

*So that ye come behind in no gift; waiting
for the coming of our Lord Jesus Christ.*
1 Corinthians 1:7

240

*For in him dwelleth all the fulness of the Godhead bodily.
And ye are complete in him, which is the head
of all principality and power.*
Colossians 2:9–10

241

*The lip of truth shall be established for ever:
but a lying tongue is but for a moment.*
Proverbs 12:19

242

*Let the wicked forsake his way, and the unrighteous
man his thoughts: and let him return unto the Lord,
and he will have mercy upon him; and to our God,
for he will abundantly pardon.*
Isaiah 55:7

243

*For ye have need of patience, that, after ye have done
the will of God, ye might receive the promise.*
Hebrews 10:36

244

*The words of a man's mouth are as deep waters,
and the wellspring of wisdom as a flowing brook.*
Proverbs 18:4

245

For I will restore health unto thee, and I will heal thee of thy wounds, saith the LORD; because they called thee an Outcast, saying, This is Zion, whom no man seeketh after.

JEREMIAH 30:17

246

And fear not them which kill the body, but are not able to kill the soul: but rather fear him which is able to destroy both soul and body in hell.

MATTHEW 10:28

247

And they said, Believe on the Lord Jesus Christ, and thou shalt be saved, and thy house.

ACTS 16:31

248

Who delivered us from so great a death, and doth deliver: in whom we trust that he will yet deliver us.

2 CORINTHIANS 1:10

249

That if thou shalt confess with thy mouth the Lord Jesus, and shalt believe in thine heart that God hath raised him from the dead, thou shalt be saved.

ROMANS 10:9

250

With long life will I satisfy him, and shew him my salvation.

PSALM 91:16

251

Ye that love the Lord, hate evil: he preserveth the souls of
his saints; he delivereth them out of the hand of the wicked.
PSALM 97:10

252

And she shall bring forth a son, and thou shalt call his
name JESUS: for he shall save his people from their sins.
MATTHEW 1:21

253

I say unto you, that likewise joy shall be in heaven over
one sinner that repenteth, more than over ninety and
nine just persons, which need no repentance.
LUKE 15:7

254

For in that he himself hath suffered being tempted,
he is able to succour them that are tempted.
HEBREWS 2:18

255

My brethren, count it all joy when ye fall into divers
temptations; knowing this, that the trying of your faith
worketh patience. But let patience have her perfect work,
that ye may be perfect and entire, wanting nothing.
JAMES 1:2–4

256

But if we walk in the light, as he is in the light,
we have fellowship one with another, and the blood
of Jesus Christ his Son cleanseth us from all sin.
1 JOHN 1:7

257

And he said, I will make all my goodness pass before thee,
and I will proclaim the name of the LORD before thee;
and will be gracious to whom I will be gracious,
and will shew mercy on whom I will shew mercy.

EXODUS 33:19

258

But he saveth the poor from the sword, from their
mouth, and from the hand of the mighty. So the poor
hath hope, and iniquity stoppeth her mouth.

JOB 5:15–16

259

When his disciples heard it, they were exceedingly amazed,
saying, Who then can be saved? But Jesus beheld them,
and said unto them, With men this is impossible;
but with God all things are possible.

MATTHEW 19:25–26

260

Behold, God is my salvation; I will trust, and not be
afraid: for the LORD JEHOVAH is my strength and
my song; he also is become my salvation.

ISAIAH 12:2

261

They that trust in the LORD shall be as mount Zion,
which cannot be removed, but abideth for ever.

PSALM 125:1

262

Come, and let us return unto the LORD:
for he hath torn, and he will heal us; he hath
smitten, and he will bind us up.

HOSEA 6:1

263

Likewise the Spirit also helpeth our infirmities: for we
know not what we should pray for as we ought: but the
Spirit itself maketh intercession for us with
groanings which cannot be uttered.

ROMANS 8:26

264

Having predestinated us unto the adoption of children by Jesus
Christ to himself, according to the good pleasure of his will.

EPHESIANS 1:5

265

For whatsoever things were written aforetime were
written for our learning, that we through patience
and comfort of the scriptures might have hope.

ROMANS 15:4

266

This then is the message which we have heard of him,
and declare unto you, that God is light,
and in him is no darkness at all.

1 JOHN 1:5

267

Fear not; for thou shalt not be ashamed: neither be thou confounded; for thou shalt not be put to shame: for thou shalt forget the shame of thy youth, and shalt not remember the reproach of thy widowhood any more.

Isaiah 54:4

268

Hope deferred maketh the heart sick: but when the desire cometh, it is a tree of life.

Proverbs 13:12

269

Behold, I shew you a mystery; We shall not all sleep, but we shall all be changed, in a moment, in the twinkling of an eye, at the last trump: for the trumpet shall sound, and the dead shall be raised incorruptible, and we shall be changed. For this corruptible must put on incorruption, and this mortal must put on immortality.

1 Corinthians 15:51–53

270

The Lord will give strength unto his people; the Lord will bless his people with peace.

Psalm 29:11

271

For God hath not given us the spirit of fear; but of power, and of love, and of a sound mind.

2 Timothy 1:7

272

For we are made partakers of Christ, if we hold the beginning of our confidence stedfast unto the end.

Hebrews 3:14

273

Let the brother of low degree rejoice in that he is exalted.
JAMES 1:9

274

And above all things have fervent charity among
yourselves: for charity shall cover the multitude of sins.
1 PETER 4:8

275

And we know that all things work together
for good to them that love God, to them who
are the called according to his purpose.
ROMANS 8:28

276

The way of the just is uprightness: thou, most upright,
dost weigh the path of the just. Yea, in the way of thy
judgments, O LORD, have we waited for thee;
the desire of our soul is to thy name,
and to the remembrance of thee.
ISAIAH 26:7–8

277

The LORD is my strength and my shield; my heart trusted
in him, and I am helped: therefore my heart greatly
rejoiceth; and with my song will I praise him.
PSALM 28:7

278

Are there any among the vanities of the Gentiles that can
cause rain? or can the heavens give showers? art not thou
he, O LORD our God? therefore we will wait upon thee:
for thou hast made all these things.
JEREMIAH 14:22

279

*Therefore whosoever heareth these sayings of mine,
and doeth them, I will liken him unto a wise man, which
built his house upon a rock: and the rain descended, and the
floods came, and the winds blew, and beat upon that
house; and it fell not: for it was founded upon a rock.*

MATTHEW 7:24–25

280

*Because the foolishness of God is wiser than men;
and the weakness of God is stronger than men.*

1 CORINTHIANS 1:25

281

*In whom ye also trusted, after that ye heard the word of
truth, the gospel of your salvation: in whom also after that
ye believed, ye were sealed with that holy Spirit of promise,
which is the earnest of our inheritance until the redemption
of the purchased possession, unto the praise of his glory.*

EPHESIANS 1:13–14

282

*Behold, what manner of love the Father hath bestowed
upon us, that we should be called the sons of God: therefore
the world knoweth us not, because it knew him not.*

1 JOHN 3:1

283

*For ye have not received the spirit of bondage again
to fear; but ye have received the Spirit of adoption,
whereby we cry, Abba, Father.*

ROMANS 8:15

284

Therefore if any man be in Christ, he is a new creature:
old things are passed away; behold, all things are become new.
2 Corinthians 5:17

285

Thou art my hiding place; thou shalt preserve me from trouble;
thou shalt compass me about with songs of deliverance.
Psalm 32:7

286

God setteth the solitary in families: he bringeth
out those which are bound with chains:
but the rebellious dwell in a dry land.
Psalm 68:6

287

At destruction and famine thou shalt laugh:
neither shalt thou be afraid of the beasts of the earth.
Job 5:22

288

Blessed be the Lord, that hath given rest unto his people
Israel, according to all that he promised: there hath not
failed one word of all his good promise, which he
promised by the hand of Moses his servant.
1 Kings 8:56

289

Rejoice not against me, O mine enemy:
when I fall, I shall arise; when I sit in darkness,
the Lord shall be a light unto me.
Micah 7:8

290

Wealth gotten by vanity shall be diminished:
but he that gathereth by labour shall increase.
PROVERBS 13:11

291

Incline your ear, and come unto me: hear, and your soul
shall live; and I will make an everlasting covenant
with you, even the sure mercies of David.
ISAIAH 55:3

292

As the living Father hath sent me, and I live by the
Father: so he that eateth me, even he shall live by me.
JOHN 6:57

293

But if the Spirit of him that raised up Jesus from the dead
dwell in you, he that raised up Christ from the dead shall also
quicken your mortal bodies by his Spirit that dwelleth in you.
ROMANS 8:11

294

The light of the body is the eye: if therefore thine eye
be single, thy whole body shall be full of light.
MATTHEW 6:22

295

For the LORD giveth wisdom: out of his mouth cometh
knowledge and understanding. He layeth up sound wisdom
for the righteous: he is a buckler to them that walk uprightly.
PROVERBS 2:6–7

296

If in this life only we have hope in Christ, we are of all men most miserable. But now is Christ risen from the dead, and become the firstfruits of them that slept.

1 Corinthians 15:19–20

297

And he said unto me, It is done. I am Alpha and Omega, the beginning and the end. I will give unto him that is athirst of the fountain of the water of life freely.

Revelation 21:6

298

But he was wounded for our transgressions, he was bruised for our iniquities: the chastisement of our peace was upon him; and with his stripes we are healed.

Isaiah 53:5

299

Fear not: for I am with thee: I will bring thy seed from the east, and gather thee from the west; I will say to the north, Give up; and to the south, Keep not back: bring my sons from far, and my daughters from the ends of the earth; even every one that is called by my name: for I have created him for my glory, I have formed him; yea, I have made him.

Isaiah 43:5–7

300

For God, who commanded the light to shine out of darkness, hath shined in our hearts, to give the light of the knowledge of the glory of God in the face of Jesus Christ.

2 Corinthians 4:6

301

For they that are after the flesh do mind the things of the flesh;
but they that are after the Spirit the things of the Spirit.
ROMANS 8:5

302

Be careful for nothing; but in every thing by prayer
and supplication with thanksgiving let your
requests be made known unto God.
PHILIPPIANS 4:6

303

But is now made manifest by the appearing of our Saviour
Jesus Christ, who hath abolished death, and hath brought
life and immortality to light through the gospel.
2 TIMOTHY 1:10

304

And this is the promise that he hath
promised us, even eternal life.
1 JOHN 2:25

305

Now faith is the substance of things hoped for,
the evidence of things not seen.
HEBREWS 11:1

306

For, behold, I create new heavens and a new earth: and the
former shall not be remembered, nor come into mind.
ISAIAH 65:17

307

O give thanks unto the LORD, for he is good:
for his mercy endureth for ever.
PSALM 107:1

308

Whom resist stedfast in the faith, knowing that the same
afflictions are accomplished in your brethren that are in the
world. But the God of all grace, who hath called us unto his
eternal glory by Christ Jesus, after that ye have suffered a
while, make you perfect, stablish, strengthen, settle you.
1 PETER 5:9–10

309

But I have trusted in thy mercy;
my heart shall rejoice in thy salvation.
PSALM 13:5

310

Commit thy works unto the LORD,
and thy thoughts shall be established.
PROVERBS 16:3

311

But unto you that fear my name shall the Sun of
righteousness arise with healing in his wings; and ye
shall go forth, and grow up as calves of the stall.
MALACHI 4:2

312

In that he saith, A new covenant, he hath made
the first old. Now that which decayeth and
waxeth old is ready to vanish away.
HEBREWS 8:13

313

*And Jesus answered and said unto her, Martha, Martha,
thou art careful and troubled about many things: but one
thing is needful: and Mary hath chosen that good part,
which shall not be taken away from her.*

LUKE 10:41–42

314

*For by grace are ye saved through faith;
and that not of yourselves: it is the gift of God.*

EPHESIANS 2:8

315

*For as many as are led by the Spirit of God,
they are the sons of God.*

ROMANS 8:14

316

*By faith the walls of Jericho fell down,
after they were compassed about seven days.*

HEBREWS 11:30

317

*He giveth power to the faint; and to them
that have no might he increaseth strength.*

ISAIAH 40:29

318

*Let not thine heart envy sinners: but be thou in the fear
of the LORD all the day long. For surely there is an end;
and thine expectation shall not be cut off.*

PROVERBS 23:17–18

319

So also is the resurrection of the dead. It is sown in corruption;
it is raised in incorruption: it is sown in dishonour; it is raised
in glory: it is sown in weakness; it is raised in power.
1 Corinthians 15:42–43

320

The highway of the upright is to depart from evil:
he that keepeth his way preserveth his soul.
Proverbs 16:17

321

Behold, they shall surely gather together,
but not by me: whosoever shall gather together
against thee shall fall for thy sake.
Isaiah 54:15

322

O give thanks unto the Lord; for he is good: for his mercy
endureth for ever. O give thanks unto the God of gods:
for his mercy endureth for ever. O give thanks to the
Lord of lords: for his mercy endureth for ever.
Psalm 136:1–3

323

And I will give them one heart, and I will put a new spirit
within you; and I will take the stony heart out of their
flesh, and will give them an heart of flesh: that they may
walk in my statutes, and keep mine ordinances, and do
them: and they shall be my people, and I will be their God.
Ezekiel 11:19–20

324

*Therefore take no thought, saying, What shall we eat? or,
What shall we drink? or, Wherewithal shall we be clothed?
(For after all these things do the Gentiles seek:) for your
heavenly Father knoweth that ye have need of all these things.*
MATTHEW 6:31–32

325

*For which cause we faint not; but though our outward
man perish, yet the inward man is renewed day by day.
For our light affliction, which is but for a moment, worketh
for us a far more exceeding and eternal weight of glory.*
2 CORINTHIANS 4:16–17

326

*Those things, which ye have both learned,
and received, and heard, and seen in me, do:
and the God of peace shall be with you.*
PHILIPPIANS 4:9

327

*My sheep hear my voice, and I know them, and they follow
me: and I give unto them eternal life; and they shall never
perish, neither shall any man pluck them out of my hand.*
JOHN 10:27–28

328

*Dearly beloved, avenge not yourselves, but rather give
place unto wrath: for it is written, Vengeance
is mine; I will repay, saith the Lord.*
ROMANS 12:19

329

And ye now therefore have sorrow:
but I will see you again, and your heart shall
rejoice, and your joy no man taketh from you.
JOHN 16:22

330

And they shall teach no more every man his neighbour,
and every man his brother, saying, Know the LORD: for
they shall all know me, from the least of them unto the
greatest of them, saith the LORD: for I will forgive their
iniquity, and I will remember their sin no more.
JEREMIAH 31:34

331

And all thy children shall be taught of the LORD;
and great shall be the peace of thy children.
ISAIAH 54:13

332

The LORD shall preserve thy going out and thy coming
in from this time forth, and even for evermore.
PSALM 121:8

333

When a wicked man dieth, his expectation shall perish:
and the hope of unjust men perisheth. The righteous
is delivered out of trouble.
PROVERBS 11:7–8

334

*Many sorrows shall be to the wicked: but he that trusteth
in the LORD, mercy shall compass him about.*

PSALM 32:10

335

But he that shall endure unto the end, the same shall be saved.

MATTHEW 24:13

336

*Much more then, being now justified by his blood,
we shall be saved from wrath through him.*

ROMANS 5:9

337

*And now abideth faith, hope, charity, these three;
but the greatest of these is charity.*

1 CORINTHIANS 13:13

338

*But without faith it is impossible to please him: for he that
cometh to God must believe that he is, and that he is a
rewarder of them that diligently seek him.*

HEBREWS 11:6

339

*And every man that hath this hope in him purifieth
himself, even as he is pure.*

1 JOHN 3:3

340

*And when they bring you unto the synagogues, and unto
magistrates, and powers, take ye no thought how or what
thing ye shall answer, or what ye shall say: for the Holy
Ghost shall teach you in the same hour what ye ought to say.*

Luke 12:11–12

341

*He loveth righteousness and judgment:
the earth is full of the goodness of the Lord.*

Psalm 33:5

342

*All the earth shall worship thee,
and shall sing unto thee; they shall sing to thy name.*

Psalm 66:4

343

*Hear therefore, O Israel, and observe to do it; that it may
be well with thee, and that ye may increase mightily,
as the Lord God of thy fathers hath promised thee,
in the land that floweth with milk and honey.*

Deuteronomy 6:3

344

*Be ye strong therefore, and let not your hands
be weak: for your work shall be rewarded.*

2 Chronicles 15:7

345

*The eternal God is thy refuge, and underneath are
the everlasting arms: and he shall thrust out the enemy
from before thee; and shall say, Destroy them.*

Deuteronomy 33:27

346

Thou shalt come to thy grave in a full age,
like as a shock of corn cometh in in his season.
JOB 5:26

347

The fear of the LORD is the beginning of wisdom:
and the knowledge of the holy is understanding.
PROVERBS 9:10

348

Thou art wearied in the greatness of thy way; yet saidst
thou not, There is no hope: thou hast found the life of
thine hand; therefore thou wast not grieved.
ISAIAH 57:10

349

Verily, verily, I say unto you,
He that believeth on me hath everlasting life.
JOHN 6:47

350

And we desire that every one of you do shew the same
diligence to the full assurance of hope unto the end: that ye
be not slothful, but followers of them who through
faith and patience inherit the promises.
HEBREWS 6:11–12

351

Whose adorning let it not be that outward adorning of
plaiting the hair, and of wearing of gold, or of putting on
of apparel; but let it be the hidden man of the heart, in that
which is not corruptible, even the ornament of a meek and
quiet spirit, which is in the sight of God of great price.
1 PETER 3:3–4

352

And who is he that will harm you, if ye
be followers of that which is good?
1 Peter 3:13

353

Behold, the Lord God will come with strong hand, and his
arm shall rule for him: behold, his reward is with him, and his
work before him. He shall feed his flock like a shepherd: he shall
gather the lambs with his arm, and carry them in his bosom,
and shall gently lead those that are with young.
Isaiah 40:10–11

354

Search the scriptures; for in them ye think ye have
eternal life: and they are they which testify of me.
John 5:39

355

The Lord is good to all: and his tender
mercies are over all his works.
Psalm 145:9

356

For the rod of the wicked shall not rest upon the lot of the
righteous; lest the righteous put forth their hands unto iniquity.
Psalm 125:3

357

Take heed that ye do not your alms before men, to be seen of them: otherwise ye have no reward of your Father which is in heaven. Therefore when thou doest thine alms, do not sound a trumpet before thee, as the hypocrites do in the synagogues and in the streets, that they may have glory of men. Verily I say unto you, They have their reward. But when thou doest alms, let not thy left hand know what thy right hand doeth: that thine alms may be in secret: and thy Father which seeth in secret himself shall reward thee openly.

MATTHEW 6:1–4

358

Behold, the LORD's hand is not shortened, that it cannot save; neither his ear heavy, that it cannot hear.

ISAIAH 59:1

359

In righteousness shalt thou be established: thou shalt be far from oppression; for thou shalt not fear: and from terror; for it shall not come near thee.

ISAIAH 54:14

360

The glory of young men is their strength: and the beauty of old men is the grey head.

PROVERBS 20:29

361

He that covereth his sins shall not prosper: but whoso confesseth and forsaketh them shall have mercy.

PROVERBS 28:13

362

God is our refuge and strength, a very present help in trouble.
Therefore will not we fear, though the earth be removed,
and though the mountains be carried into the midst of the sea;
though the waters thereof roar and be troubled, though
the mountains shake with the swelling thereof.

PSALM 46:1–3

363

Then shall ye call upon me, and ye shall go and
pray unto me, and I will hearken unto you.

JEREMIAH 29:12

364

But go ye and learn what that meaneth, I will have
mercy, and not sacrifice: for I am not come to call
the righteous, but sinners to repentance.

MATTHEW 9:13

365

For I am with thee, and no man shall set on thee
to hurt thee: for I have much people in this city.

ACTS 18:10

366

Therefore I say unto you, What things soever ye desire,
when ye pray, believe that ye receive them,
and ye shall have them.

MARK 11:24

367

Be not ye therefore like unto them: for your Father knoweth
what things ye have need of, before ye ask him.

MATTHEW 6:8

368

For the creature was made subject to vanity, not willingly,
but by reason of him who hath subjected the same in hope,
because the creature itself also shall be delivered from
the bondage of corruption into the glorious
liberty of the children of God.
ROMANS 8:20–21

369

For all the promises of God in him are yea,
and in him Amen, unto the glory of God by us.
2 CORINTHIANS 1:20

370

Let us hold fast the profession of our faith without
wavering; (for he is faithful that promised).
HEBREWS 10:23

371

Marvel not at this: for the hour is coming, in the which all
that are in the graves shall hear his voice, and shall come forth;
they that have done good, unto the resurrection of life; and they
that have done evil, unto the resurrection of damnation.
JOHN 5:28–29

372

Not every one that saith unto me, Lord, Lord,
shall enter into the kingdom of heaven; but he that
doeth the will of my Father which is in heaven.
MATTHEW 7:21

373

*The king's heart is in the hand of the LORD, as the rivers
of water: he turneth it whithersoever he will.*
PROVERBS 21:1

374

*Herein is my Father glorified, that ye bear
much fruit; so shall ye be my disciples.*
JOHN 15:8

375

*Jesus saith unto him, Thomas, because thou hast seen
me, thou hast believed: blessed are they that
have not seen, and yet have believed.*
JOHN 20:29

376

*And I have declared unto them thy name,
and will declare it: that the love wherewith thou
hast loved me may be in them, and I in them.*
JOHN 17:26

377

*Thou wilt keep him in perfect peace, whose mind
is stayed on thee: because he trusteth in thee.*
ISAIAH 26:3

378

*A false balance is abomination to the LORD:
but a just weight is his delight.*
PROVERBS 11:1

379

And not only so, but we glory in tribulations also:
knowing that tribulation worketh patience.
ROMANS 5:3

380

I will abundantly bless her provision:
I will satisfy her poor with bread.
PSALM 132:15

381

Therefore I take pleasure in infirmities, in reproaches,
in necessities, in persecutions, in distresses for Christ's
sake: for when I am weak, then am I strong.
2 CORINTHIANS 12:10

382

That Christ may dwell in your hearts by faith;
that ye, being rooted and grounded in love, may be
able to comprehend with all saints what is the breadth,
and length, and depth, and height; and to know the
love of Christ, which passeth knowledge, that ye
might be filled with all the fulness of God.
EPHESIANS 3:17–19

383

But I would not have you to be ignorant, brethren,
concerning them which are asleep, that ye sorrow not,
even as others which have no hope. For if we believe
that Jesus died and rose again, even so them also
which sleep in Jesus will God bring with him.
1 THESSALONIANS 4:13–14

384

Jesus Christ the same yesterday, and to day, and for ever.
HEBREWS 13:8

385

Henceforth I call you not servants; for the servant knoweth
not what his lord doeth: but I have called you friends;
for all things that I have heard of my Father
I have made known unto you.
JOHN 15:15

386

Sell that ye have, and give alms; provide yourselves bags
which wax not old, a treasure in the heavens that faileth
not, where no thief approacheth, neither moth corrupteth.
LUKE 12:33

387

And kings shall be thy nursing fathers, and their queens
thy nursing mothers: they shall bow down to thee with
their face toward the earth, and lick up the dust of
thy feet; and thou shalt know that I am the LORD:
for they shall not be ashamed that wait for me.
ISAIAH 49:23

388

Better is a dry morsel, and quietness therewith,
than an house full of sacrifices with strife.
PROVERBS 17:1

389

Wait on the LORD: be of good courage, and he shall
strengthen thine heart: wait, I say, on the LORD.
PSALM 27:14

390

But seek ye first the kingdom of God, and his righteousness;
and all these things shall be added unto you.
MATTHEW 6:33

391

Verily, verily, I say unto you, That ye shall weep and
lament, but the world shall rejoice: and ye shall be
sorrowful, but your sorrow shall be turned into joy.
JOHN 16:20

392

Give, and it shall be given unto you; good measure, pressed
down, and shaken together, and running over, shall men
give into your bosom. For with the same measure that ye
mete withal it shall be measured to you again.
LUKE 6:38

393

Watch ye, stand fast in the faith,
quit you like men, be strong.
1 CORINTHIANS 16:13

394

He that goeth forth and weepeth, bearing precious
seed, shall doubtless come again with rejoicing,
bringing his sheaves with him.
PSALM 126:6

395

Thy righteousness is like the great mountains;
thy judgments are a great deep: O LORD,
thou preservest man and beast.
PSALM 36:6

396

But if from thence thou shalt seek the Lord thy God,
thou shalt find him, if thou seek him with
all thy heart and with all thy soul.
Deuteronomy 4:29

397

If iniquity be in thine hand, put it far away,
and let not wickedness dwell in thy tabernacles.
For then shalt thou lift up thy face without spot;
yea, thou shalt be stedfast, and shalt not fear.
Job 11:14–15

398

And all things, whatsoever ye shall ask
in prayer, believing, ye shall receive.
Matthew 21:22

399

The Lord upholdeth all that fall,
and raiseth up all those that be bowed down.
Psalm 145:14

400

Therefore the redeemed of the Lord shall return, and come
with singing unto Zion; and everlasting joy shall be
upon their head: they shall obtain gladness and joy;
and sorrow and mourning shall flee away.
Isaiah 51:11

401

Ye have not chosen me, but I have chosen you, and ordained you, that ye should go and bring forth fruit, and that your fruit should remain: that whatsoever ye shall ask of the Father in my name, he may give it you.

JOHN 15:16

402

Evening, and morning, and at noon, will I pray, and cry aloud: and he shall hear my voice.

PSALM 55:17

403

But it is good for me to draw near to God: I have put my trust in the Lord God, that I may declare all thy works.

PSALM 73:28

404

And ye shall seek me, and find me, when ye shall search for me with all your heart.

JEREMIAH 29:13

405

Jesus said unto him, If thou wilt be perfect, go and sell that thou hast, and give to the poor, and thou shalt have treasure in heaven: and come and follow me.

MATTHEW 19:21

406

The Spirit itself beareth witness with our spirit, that we are the children of God: and if children, then heirs; heirs of God, and joint-heirs with Christ; if so be that we suffer with him, that we may be also glorified together.

ROMANS 8:16–17

407

Yea doubtless, and I count all things but loss for the
excellency of the knowledge of Christ Jesus my Lord:
for whom I have suffered the loss of all things, and do
count them but dung, that I may win Christ.
Philippians 3:8

408

But the natural man receiveth not the things of the Spirit
of God: for they are foolishness unto him: neither can he
know them, because they are spiritually discerned.
But he that is spiritual judgeth all things,
yet he himself is judged of no man.
1 Corinthians 2:14–15

409

Cast not away therefore your confidence,
which hath great recompence of reward.
Hebrews 10:35

410

And now, little children, abide in him; that,
when he shall appear, we may have confidence,
and not be ashamed before him at his coming.
1 John 2:28

411

All we like sheep have gone astray; we have
turned every one to his own way; and the Lord
hath laid on him the iniquity of us all.
Isaiah 53:6

412

*Blessed is the man that trusteth in the L*ORD*, and whose hope the Lord is. For he shall be as a tree planted by the waters, and that spreadeth out her roots by the river, and shall not see when heat cometh, but her leaf shall be green; and shall not be careful in the year of drought, neither shall cease from yielding fruit.*

JEREMIAH 17:7–8

413

All the days of the afflicted are evil: but he that is of a merry heart hath a continual feast.

PROVERBS 15:15

414

He that believeth on him is not condemned: but he that believeth not is condemned already, because he hath not believed in the name of the only begotten Son of God.

JOHN 3:18

415

As many as I love, I rebuke and chasten: be zealous therefore, and repent.

REVELATION 3:19

416

Through faith also Sara herself received strength to conceive seed, and was delivered of a child when she was past age, because she judged him faithful who had promised.

HEBREWS 11:11

417

But whosoever drinketh of the water that I shall give him shall never thirst; but the water that I shall give him shall be in him a well of water springing up into everlasting life.

JOHN 4:14

418

Sow to yourselves in righteousness, reap in mercy; break up your fallow ground: for it is time to seek the LORD, till he come and rain righteousness upon you.

HOSEA 10:12

419

The name of the Lord is a strong tower: the righteous runneth into it, and is safe.

PROVERBS 18:10

420

Ointment and perfume rejoice the heart: so doth the sweetness of a man's friend by hearty counsel.

PROVERBS 27:9

421

And to love him with all the heart, and with all the understanding, and with all the soul, and with all the strength, and to love his neighbour as himself, is more than all whole burnt offerings and sacrifices.

MARK 12:33

422

He that keepeth the commandment keepeth his own soul;
but he that despiseth his ways shall die.
PROVERBS 19:16

423

Bless the LORD, O my soul, and forget not all his benefits:
who forgiveth all thine iniquities; who healeth all thy
diseases; who redeemeth thy life from destruction; who
crowneth thee with lovingkindness and tender mercies.
PSALM 103:2–4

424

No weapon that is formed against thee shall prosper; and
every tongue that shall rise against thee in judgment thou
shalt condemn. This is the heritage of the servants of the
LORD, and their righteousness is of me, saith the LORD.
ISAIAH 54:17

425

In the day when I cried thou answeredst me,
and strengthenedst me with strength in my soul.
PSALM 138:3

426

Now therefore ye are no more strangers and foreigners,
but fellowcitizens with the saints, and of the household of God.
EPHESIANS 2:19

427

But God hath chosen the foolish things of the world to confound the wise; and God hath chosen the weak things of the world to confound the things which are mighty; and base things of the world, and things which are despised, hath God chosen, yea, and things which are not, to bring to nought things that are: that no flesh should glory in his presence. But of him are ye in Christ Jesus, who of God is made unto us wisdom, and righteousness, and sanctification, and redemption.

1 Corinthians 1:27–30

428

Therefore, brethren, we are debtors, not to the flesh, to live after the flesh. For if ye live after the flesh, ye shall die: but if ye through the Spirit do mortify the deeds of the body, ye shall live.

Romans 8:12–13

429

So that we may boldly say, The Lord is my helper, and I will not fear what man shall do unto me.

Hebrews 13:6

430

Praise ye the Lord. Blessed is the man that feareth the Lord, that delighteth greatly in his commandments. . . . Wealth and riches shall be in his house: and his righteousness endureth for ever.

Psalm 112:1, 3

431

Only fear the Lord, and serve him in truth with all your heart: for consider how great things he hath done for you.

1 Samuel 12:24

432

Remember ye not the former things, neither consider the things of old. Behold, I will do a new thing; now it shall spring forth; shall ye not know it? I will even make a way in the wilderness, and rivers in the desert.

ISAIAH 43:18–19

433

The angel of the LORD encampeth round about them that fear him, and delivereth them.

PSALM 34:7

434

For thou art my hope, O Lord God: thou art my trust from my youth.

PSALM 71:5

435

A little that a righteous man hath is better than the riches of many wicked.

PSALM 37:16

436

As far as the east is from the west, so far hath he removed our transgressions from us.

PSALM 103:12

437

Blessed are they which do hunger and thirst after righteousness: for they shall be filled.

MATTHEW 5:6

438

The hope of the righteous shall be gladness:
but the expectation of the wicked shall perish.
PROVERBS 10:28

439

That they should seek the Lord, if haply they might feel after
him, and find him, though he be not far from every one of us.
ACTS 17:27

440

Who against hope believed in hope, that he might
become the father of many nations, according to
that which was spoken, So shall thy seed be.
ROMANS 4:18

441

My soul, wait thou only upon God;
for my expectation is from him.
PSALM 62:5

442

For ye shall go out with joy, and be led forth with peace:
the mountains and the hills shall break forth before you into
singing, and all the trees of the field shall clap their hands.
ISAIAH 55:12

443

God is not a man, that he should lie; neither the son of
man, that he should repent: hath he said, and shall he not
do it? or hath he spoken, and shall he not make it good?
NUMBERS 23:19

444

*And it shall come to pass, that before they call, I will
answer; and while they are yet speaking, I will hear.*
Isaiah 65:24

445

*Verily, verily, I say unto you, If a man keep
my saying, he shall never see death.*
John 8:51

446

*Beloved, let us love one another: for love is of God; and
every one that loveth is born of God, and knoweth God.*
1 John 4:7

447

*For thus saith the high and lofty One that inhabiteth eternity,
whose name is Holy; I dwell in the high and holy place, with
him also that is of a contrite and humble spirit, to revive the
spirit of the humble, and to revive the heart of the contrite ones.*
Isaiah 57:15

448

*The young lions do lack, and suffer hunger: but they
that seek the Lord shall not want any good thing.*
Psalm 34:10

449

*Though ye have lien among the pots, yet shall ye be
as the wings of a dove covered with silver,
and her feathers with yellow gold.*
Psalm 68:13

450

And of Benjamin he said, The beloved of the LORD shall dwell in safety by him; and the Lord shall cover him all the day long, and he shall dwell between his shoulders.

DEUTERONOMY 33:12

451

If, when evil cometh upon us, as the sword, judgment, or pestilence, or famine, we stand before this house, and in thy presence, (for thy name is in this house,) and cry unto thee in our affliction, then thou wilt hear and help.

2 CHRONICLES 20:9

452

The integrity of the upright shall guide them: but the perverseness of transgressors shall destroy them.

PROVERBS 11:3

453

(For the LORD thy God is a merciful God;) he will not forsake thee, neither destroy thee, nor forget the covenant of thy fathers which he sware unto them.

DEUTERONOMY 4:31

454

And the King shall answer and say unto them, Verily I say unto you, Inasmuch as ye have done it unto one of the least of these my brethren, ye have done it unto me.

MATTHEW 25:40

455

But go thou thy way till the end be: for thou shalt rest, and stand in thy lot at the end of the days.

DANIEL 12:13

456

My soul melteth for heaviness: strengthen
thou me according unto thy word.

PSALM 119:28

457

The LORD shall preserve thee from all evil:
he shall preserve thy soul.

PSALM 121:7

458

And he answered, Fear not: for they that be with
us are more than they that be with them.

2 KINGS 6:16

459

And thine age shall be clearer than the noonday:
thou shalt shine forth, thou shalt be as the morning.

JOB 11:17

460

And he will love thee, and bless thee, and multiply thee:
he will also bless the fruit of thy womb, and the fruit of thy
land, thy corn, and thy wine, and thine oil, the increase of
thy kine, and the flocks of thy sheep, in the land which
he sware unto thy fathers to give thee.

DEUTERONOMY 7:13

461

Hearken, my beloved brethren, Hath not God chosen the
poor of this world rich in faith, and heirs of the kingdom
which he hath promised to them that love him?

JAMES 2:5

462

For God is not unrighteous to forget your work and labour of love, which ye have shewed toward his name, in that ye have ministered to the saints, and do minister.
HEBREWS 6:10

463

Fret not thyself because of evildoers, neither be thou envious against the workers of iniquity. For they shall soon be cut down like the grass, and wither as the green herb.
PSALM 37:1–2

464

Therefore they shall come and sing in the height of Zion, and shall flow together to the goodness of the LORD, for wheat, and for wine, and for oil, and for the young of the flock and of the herd: and their soul shall be as a watered garden; and they shall not sorrow any more at all.
JEREMIAH 31:12

465

The LORD shall cause thine enemies that rise up against thee to be smitten before thy face: they shall come out against thee one way, and flee before thee seven ways.
DEUTERONOMY 28:7

466

And I say also unto thee, That thou art Peter, and upon this rock I will build my church; and the gates of hell shall not prevail against it.
MATTHEW 16:18

467

That the blessing of Abraham might come on the Gentiles through Jesus Christ; that we might receive the promise of the Spirit through faith.
GALATIANS 3:14

468

Trust in the LORD with all thine heart; and lean not unto thine own understanding. In all thy ways acknowledge him, and he shall direct thy paths.
PROVERBS 3:5–6

469

For ye know the grace of our Lord Jesus Christ, that, though he was rich, yet for your sakes he became poor, that ye through his poverty might be rich.
2 CORINTHIANS 8:9

470

Ye have put off the old man with his deeds; and have put on the new man, which is renewed in knowledge after the image of him that created him.
COLOSSIANS 3:9–10

471

He hath given meat unto them that fear him: he will ever be mindful of his covenant.
PSALM 111:5

472

To every thing there is a season, and a time to every purpose under the heaven.
ECCLESIASTES 3:1

473

But the LORD is my defence;
and my God is the rock of my refuge.
PSALM 94:22

474

Whereby are given unto us exceeding great and precious
promises: that by these ye might be partakers of the
divine nature, having escaped the corruption
that is in the world through lust.
2 PETER 1:4

475

Beloved, think it not strange concerning the fiery trial
which is to try you, as though some strange thing happened
unto you: but rejoice, inasmuch as ye are partakers of
Christ's sufferings; that, when his glory shall be revealed,
ye may be glad also with exceeding joy.
1 PETER 4:12–13

476

Righteousness exalteth a nation:
but sin is a reproach to any people.
PROVERBS 14:34

477

See, I have set before thee this day life and good, and death
and evil; in that I command thee this day to love the LORD
thy God, to walk in his ways, and to keep his commandments
and his statutes and his judgments, that thou mayest live
and multiply: and the LORD thy God shall bless thee in
the land whither thou goest to possess it.
DEUTERONOMY 30:15–16

478

And he said unto him, Son, thou art ever with me,
and all that I have is thine.

LUKE 15:31

479

For as by one man's disobedience many were made sinners,
so by the obedience of one shall many be made righteous.

ROMANS 5:19

480

He that trusteth in his riches shall fall;
but the righteous shall flourish as a branch.

PROVERBS 11:28

481

But as for me, I will come into thy house in
the multitude of thy mercy: and in thy fear
will I worship toward thy holy temple.

PSALM 5:7

482

If any man's work shall be burned, he shall suffer loss:
but he himself shall be saved; yet so as by fire.

1 CORINTHIANS 3:15

483

For by one offering he hath perfected for
ever them that are sanctified.

HEBREWS 10:14

484

*But ye are a chosen generation, a royal priesthood, an holy
nation, a peculiar people; that ye should shew forth the
praises of him who hath called you out of darkness
into his marvellous light.*

1 PETER 2:9

485

*And whatsoever we ask, we receive of him,
because we keep his commandments, and do
those things that are pleasing in his sight.*

1 JOHN 3:22

486

*Lift up your eyes to the heavens, and look upon the earth
beneath: for the heavens shall vanish away like smoke,
and the earth shall wax old like a garment, and they that
dwell therein shall die in like manner: but my salvation
shall be for ever, and my righteousness shall not be abolished.*

ISAIAH 51:6

487

*Know therefore this day, and consider it in thine heart,
that the LORD he is God in heaven above, and upon
the earth beneath: there is none else.*

DEUTERONOMY 4:39

488

*And also the Strength of Israel will not lie nor repent:
for he is not a man, that he should repent.*

1 SAMUEL 15:29

489

*Yea, I will rejoice over them to do them good,
and I will plant them in this land assuredly with
my whole heart and with my whole soul.*
JEREMIAH 32:41

490

*When he maketh inquisition for blood, he remembereth
them: he forgetteth not the cry of the humble.*
PSALM 9:12

491

*Cast thy burden upon the LORD, and he shall sustain thee:
he shall never suffer the righteous to be moved.*
PSALM 55:22

492

*My flesh and my heart faileth: but God is the
strength of my heart, and my portion for ever.*
PSALM 73:26

493

*Confess your faults one to another, and pray one for
another, that ye may be healed. The effectual fervent
prayer of a righteous man availeth much.*
JAMES 5:16

494

Casting all your care upon him; for he careth for you.
1 PETER 5:7

495

*For we know that if our earthly house of this tabernacle
were dissolved, we have a building of God, an house not
made with hands, eternal in the heavens.*

2 CORINTHIANS 5:1

496

*Though I walk in the midst of trouble, thou wilt revive me:
thou shalt stretch forth thine hand against the wrath
of mine enemies, and thy right hand shall save me.*

PSALM 138:7

497

*He found him in a desert land, and in the waste
howling wilderness; he led him about, he instructed
him, he kept him as the apple of his eye.*

DEUTERONOMY 32:10

498

*I will ransom them from the power of the grave;
I will redeem them from death: O death, I will be
thy plagues; O grave, I will be thy destruction:
repentance shall be hid from mine eyes.*

HOSEA 13:14

499

I will not leave you comfortless: I will come to you.

JOHN 14:18

500

As the Father hath loved me, so have I loved you:
continue ye in my love. If ye keep my commandments,
ye shall abide in my love; even as I have kept my Father's
commandments, and abide in his love. These things have
I spoken unto you, that my joy might remain in you,
and that your joy might be full.

JOHN 15:9–11

501

Because he hath set his love upon me, therefore
will I deliver him: I will set him on high,
because he hath known my name.

PSALM 91:14

502

Knowing this, that our old man is crucified with him,
that the body of sin might be destroyed, that henceforth we
should not serve sin. For he that is dead is freed from sin.

ROMANS 6:6–7

503

The eyes of the LORD are in every place,
beholding the evil and the good.

PROVERBS 15:3

504

The humble shall see this, and be glad:
and your heart shall live that seek God.

PSALM 69:32

505

The lines are fallen unto me in pleasant places;
yea, I have a goodly heritage.
PSALM 16:6

506

Nay, in all these things we are more than conquerors through
him that loved us. For I am persuaded, that neither death,
nor life, nor angels, nor principalities, nor powers, nor things
present, nor things to come, nor height, nor depth, nor any
other creature, shall be able to separate us from the love
of God, which is in Christ Jesus our Lord.
ROMANS 8:37–39

507

Honour thy father and mother; which is the first
commandment with promise; that it may be well
with thee, and thou mayest live long on the earth.
EPHESIANS 6:2–3

508

Fear not, little flock; for it is your Father's
good pleasure to give you the kingdom.
LUKE 12:32

509

But thus saith the LORD, Even the captives of the mighty
shall be taken away, and the prey of the terrible shall be
delivered: for I will contend with him that contendeth
with thee, and I will save thy children.
ISAIAH 49:25

510

The fear of the wicked, it shall come upon him:
but the desire of the righteous shall be granted.
PROVERBS 10:24

511

But my God shall supply all your need according
to his riches in glory by Christ Jesus.
PHILIPPIANS 4:19

512

For as in Adam all die, even so in
Christ shall all be made alive.
1 CORINTHIANS 15:22

513

For if our heart condemn us, God is greater
than our heart, and knoweth all things.
1 JOHN 3:20

514

The steps of a good man are ordered by the LORD:
and he delighteth in his way.
PSALM 37:23

515

Be strong and of a good courage, fear not, nor be afraid
of them: for the LORD thy God, he it is that doth go
with thee; he will not fail thee, nor forsake thee.
DEUTERONOMY 31:6

516

He shall not be afraid of evil tidings:
his heart is fixed, trusting in the LORD.
PSALM 112:7

517

As a shepherd seeketh out his flock in the day that he is among his sheep that are scattered; so will I seek out my sheep, and will deliver them out of all places where they have been scattered in the cloudy and dark day.

Ezekiel 34:12

518

Thou hast seen it; for thou beholdest mischief and spite, to requite it with thy hand: the poor committeth himself unto thee; thou art the helper of the fatherless.

Psalm 10:14

519

So that a man shall say, Verily there is a reward for the righteous: verily he is a God that judgeth in the earth.

Psalm 58:11

520

For I have said, Mercy shall be built up for ever: thy faithfulness shalt thou establish in the very heavens.

Psalm 89:2

521

For if ye forgive men their trespasses, your heavenly Father will also forgive you.

Matthew 6:14

522

For the righteous Lord loveth righteousness; his countenance doth behold the upright.

Psalm 11:7

523

And he that keepeth his commandments dwelleth in him,
and he in him. And hereby we know that he abideth
in us, by the Spirit which he hath given us.

1 JOHN 3:24

524

As newborn babes, desire the sincere milk
of the word, that ye may grow thereby.

1 PETER 2:2

525

The LORD hath appeared of old unto me, saying, Yea,
I have loved thee with an everlasting love: therefore
with lovingkindness have I drawn thee.

JEREMIAH 31:3

526

Howbeit when he, the Spirit of truth, is come, he will
guide you into all truth: for he shall not speak of himself;
but whatsoever he shall hear, that shall he speak:
and he will shew you things to come.

JOHN 16:13

527

Thou openest thine hand, and satisfiest
the desire of every living thing.

PSALM 145:16

528

Who hath ascended up into heaven, or descended? who hath
gathered the wind in his fists? who hath bound the waters
in a garment? who hath established all the ends of the earth?
what is his name, and what is his son's name, if thou canst
tell? Every word of God is pure: he is a shield
unto them that put their trust in him.

PROVERBS 30:4–5

529

But when thou makest a feast, call the poor, the maimed,
the lame, the blind: and thou shalt be blessed; for they
cannot recompense thee: for thou shalt be recompensed
at the resurrection of the just.

LUKE 14:13–14

530

The LORD hath prepared his throne in the heavens;
and his kingdom ruleth over all.

PSALM 103:19

531

The blessing of the LORD, it maketh rich,
and he addeth no sorrow with it.

PROVERBS 10:22

532

His heart is established, he shall not be afraid,
until he see his desire upon his enemies.

PSALM 112:8

533

And now come I to thee; and these things I speak in the
world, that they might have my joy fulfilled in themselves.

JOHN 17:13

534

Know ye not that ye are the temple of God,
and that the Spirit of God dwelleth in you?
1 CORINTHIANS 3:16

535

LORD, thou hast heard the desire of the humble: thou wilt
prepare their heart, thou wilt cause thine ear to hear.
PSALM 10:17

536

But God will redeem my soul from the power
of the grave: for he shall receive me.
PSALM 49:15

537

Ye shall walk in all the ways which the LORD your
God hath commanded you, that ye may live, and that
it may be well with you, and that ye may prolong
your days in the land which ye shall possess.
DEUTERONOMY 5:33

538

For the LORD heareth the poor,
and despiseth not his prisoners.
PSALM 69:33

539

For the LORD God is a sun and shield: the LORD
will give grace and glory: no good thing will he
withhold from them that walk uprightly.
PSALM 84:11

540

Behold, thou desirest truth in the inward parts: and in the hidden part thou shalt make me to know wisdom.

<small>PSALM 51:6</small>

541

Behold, he that keepeth Israel shall neither slumber nor sleep.

<small>PSALM 121:4</small>

542

Therefore now let it please thee to bless the house of thy servant, that it may continue for ever before thee: for thou, O Lord God, hast spoken it: and with thy blessing let the house of thy servant be blessed for ever.

<small>2 SAMUEL 7:29</small>

543

And though after my skin worms destroy this body, yet in my flesh shall I see God: whom I shall see for myself, and mine eyes shall behold, and not another; though my reins be consumed within me.

<small>JOB 19:26–27</small>

544

Let the field be joyful, and all that is therein: then shall all the trees of the wood rejoice before the LORD: for he cometh, for he cometh to judge the earth: he shall judge the world with righteousness, and the people with his truth.

<small>PSALM 96:12–13</small>

545

I in them, and thou in me, that they may be made perfect in one; and that the world may know that thou hast sent me, and hast loved them, as thou hast loved me.

JOHN 17:23

546

He healeth the broken in heart, and bindeth up their wounds.

PSALM 147:3

547

I the LORD have called thee in righteousness, and will hold thine hand, and will keep thee, and give thee for a covenant of the people, for a light of the Gentiles; to open the blind eyes, to bring out the prisoners from the prison, and them that sit in darkness out of the prison house.

ISAIAH 42:6–7

548

But the righteousness which is of faith speaketh on this wise, Say not in thine heart, Who shall ascend into heaven? (that is, to bring Christ down from above:) or, Who shall descend into the deep? (that is, to bring up Christ again from the dead.) But what saith it? The word is nigh thee, even in thy mouth, and in thy heart: that is, the word of faith, which we preach.

ROMANS 10:6–8

549

For ye are all the children of God by faith in Christ Jesus.

GALATIANS 3:26

550

*How much more shall the blood of Christ, who through the
eternal Spirit offered himself without spot to God, purge
your conscience from dead works to serve the living God?*

HEBREWS 9:14

551

*The righteous cry, and the LORD heareth,
and delivereth them out of all their troubles.*

PSALM 34:17

552

*Why sayest thou, O Jacob, and speakest, O Israel,
My way is hid from the Lord, and my judgment is passed
over from my God? Hast thou not known? hast thou not
heard, that the everlasting God, the Lord, the Creator of
the ends of the earth, fainteth not, neither is weary?
there is no searching of his understanding.*

ISAIAH 40:27–28

553

*And it shall be to me a name of joy, a praise and an honour
before all the nations of the earth, which shall hear all the good
that I do unto them: and they shall fear and tremble for all the
goodness and for all the prosperity that I procure unto it.*

JEREMIAH 33:9

554

*The labour of the righteous tendeth to life:
the fruit of the wicked to sin.*

PROVERBS 10:16

555

Ye that fear the LORD, trust in the LORD:
he is their help and their shield.
PSALM 115:11

556

Because thou shalt forget thy misery,
and remember it as waters that pass away.
JOB 11:16

557

For the needy shall not always be forgotten:
the expectation of the poor shall not perish for ever.
PSALM 9:18

558

And ye shall eat in plenty, and be satisfied, and praise the
name of the LORD your God, that hath dealt wondrously
with you: and my people shall never be ashamed.
JOEL 2:26

559

I have called upon thee, for thou wilt hear me, O God:
incline thine ear unto me, and hear my speech.
PSALM 17:6

560

The law of the LORD is perfect, converting the soul: the
testimony of the LORD is sure, making wise the simple.
PSALM 19:7

561

When my father and my mother forsake me,
then the LORD will take me up.

PSALM 27:10

562

They that dwell under his shadow shall return;
they shall revive as the corn, and grow as the vine:
the scent thereof shall be as the wine of Lebanon.

HOSEA 14:7

563

And I will bring the blind by a way that they knew not;
I will lead them in paths that they have not known: I will
make darkness light before them, and crooked things straight.
These things will I do unto them, and not forsake them.

ISAIAH 42:16

564

He hath remembered his covenant for ever, the word
which he commanded to a thousand generations.

PSALM 105:8

565

Every good gift and every perfect gift is from above,
and cometh down from the Father of lights, with whom
is no variableness, neither shadow of turning.

JAMES 1:17

566

Yet setteth he the poor on high from affliction,
and maketh him families like a flock.

PSALM 107:41

567

*Do they not err that devise evil? but mercy
and truth shall be to them that devise good.*

PROVERBS 14:22

568

*And, Thou, Lord, in the beginning hast laid the foundation
of the earth; and the heavens are the works of thine hands:
they shall perish; but thou remainest; and they all shall
wax old as doth a garment; and as a vesture shalt thou
fold them up, and they shall be changed: but thou art
the same, and thy years shall not fail.*

HEBREWS 1:10–12

569

*Blessed be the God and Father of our Lord Jesus Christ, which
according to his abundant mercy hath begotten us again unto
a lively hope by the resurrection of Jesus Christ from the dead,
to an inheritance incorruptible, and undefiled, and that
fadeth not away, reserved in heaven for you, who are kept
by the power of God through faith unto salvation
ready to be revealed in the last time.*

1 PETER 1:3–5

570

*Wherefore he is able also to save them to the
uttermost that come unto God by him, seeing he
ever liveth to make intercession for them.*

HEBREWS 7:25

571

*The way of the slothful man is as an hedge of thorns:
but the way of the righteous is made plain.*

PROVERBS 15:19

572

*Trust in the LORD, and do good; so shalt thou dwell
in the land, and verily thou shalt be fed.*
PSALM 37:3

573

*For the which cause I also suffer these things: nevertheless
I am not ashamed: for I know whom I have believed,
and am persuaded that he is able to keep that which
I have committed unto him against that day.*
2 TIMOTHY 1:12

574

*And we have known and believed the love that
God hath to us. God is love; and he that dwelleth
in love dwelleth in God, and God in him.*
1 JOHN 4:16

575

*Blessed is he that readeth, and they that hear the
words of this prophecy, and keep those things which
are written therein: for the time is at hand.*
REVELATION 1:3

576

*My soul shall be satisfied as with marrow and fatness;
and my mouth shall praise thee with joyful lips.*
PSALM 63:5

577

*The righteous shall be glad in the Lord, and shall trust
in him; and all the upright in heart shall glory.*
PSALM 64:10

578

Wherefore it shall come to pass, if ye hearken to these judgments, and keep, and do them, that the LORD thy God shall keep unto thee the covenant and the mercy which he sware unto thy fathers.

DEUTERONOMY 7:12

579

And have hope toward God, which they themselves also allow, that there shall be a resurrection of the dead, both of the just and unjust.

ACTS 24:15

580

Also now, behold, my witness is in heaven, and my record is on high.

JOB 16:19

581

Nevertheless I am continually with thee: thou hast holden me by my right hand. Thou shalt guide me with thy counsel, and afterward receive me to glory.

PSALM 73:23–24

582

For this God is our God for ever and ever: he will be our guide even unto death.

PSALM 48:14

583

For as the sufferings of Christ abound in us, so our consolation also aboundeth by Christ.

2 CORINTHIANS 1:5

584

*Delight thyself also in the LORD: and he shall
give thee the desires of thine heart.*

PSALM 37:4

585

*Neither is there any creature that is not manifest in
his sight: but all things are naked and opened unto
the eyes of him with whom we have to do.*

HEBREWS 4:13

586

*Thou wilt shew me the path of life: in thy presence is fulness
of joy; at thy right hand there are pleasures for evermore.*

PSALM 16:11

587

*Thou shalt surely give him, and thine heart shall not be
grieved when thou givest unto him: because that for this
thing the LORD thy God shall bless thee in all thy works,
and in all that thou puttest thine hand unto.*

DEUTERONOMY 15:10

588

*Take therefore no thought for the morrow:
for the morrow shall take thought for the things of
itself. Sufficient unto the day is the evil thereof.*

MATTHEW 6:34

589

*Moreover the law entered, that the offence might abound.
But where sin abounded, grace did much more abound: that as
sin hath reigned unto death, even so might grace reign through
righteousness unto eternal life by Jesus Christ our Lord.*

ROMANS 5:20–21

590

*The LORD trieth the righteous: but the wicked
and him that loveth violence his soul hateth.*

PSALM 11:5

591

*And I will cleanse them from all their iniquity, whereby
they have sinned against me; and I will pardon all their
iniquities, whereby they have sinned, and whereby
they have transgressed against me.*

JEREMIAH 33:8

592

*I am the good shepherd, and know my sheep, and am
known of mine. As the Father knoweth me, even so know I
the Father: and I lay down my life for the sheep. And other
sheep I have, which are not of this fold: them also I must
bring, and they shall hear my voice; and there
shall be one fold, and one shepherd.*

JOHN 10:14–16

593

*For sin shall not have dominion over you:
for ye are not under the law, but under grace.*

ROMANS 6:14

594

*For whom the LORD loveth he correcteth;
even as a father the son in whom he delighteth.*

PROVERBS 3:12

595

*The LORD is the portion of mine inheritance
and of my cup: thou maintainest my lot.*

PSALM 16:5

596

*His lord said unto him, Well done, thou good and faithful
servant: thou hast been faithful over a few things,
I will make thee ruler over many things:
enter thou into the joy of thy lord.*

MATTHEW 25:21

597

*For the Father himself loveth you, because ye have loved
me, and have believed that I came out from God.*

JOHN 16:27

598

*Wherefore seeing we also are compassed about with so great
a cloud of witnesses, let us lay aside every weight, and the sin
which doth so easily beset us, and let us run with patience the
race that is set before us, looking unto Jesus the author and
finisher of our faith; who for the joy that was set before him
endured the cross, despising the shame, and is set down
at the right hand of the throne of God.*

HEBREWS 12:1–2

599

*Yet if any man suffer as a Christian, let him not be
ashamed; but let him glorify God on this behalf.*

1 PETER 4:16

600

*He hath dispersed, he hath given to the poor;
his righteousness endureth for ever;
his horn shall be exalted with honour.*

PSALM 112:9

601

When thou liest down, thou shalt not be afraid:
yea, thou shalt lie down, and thy sleep shall be sweet.
PROVERBS 3:24

602

I have seen an end of all perfection:
but thy commandment is exceeding broad.
PSALM 119:96

603

Till he fill thy mouth with laughing,
and thy lips with rejoicing.
JOB 8:21

604

For the LORD your God is he that goeth with you,
to fight for you against your enemies, to save you.
DEUTERONOMY 20:4

605

The earth and all the inhabitants thereof
are dissolved: I bear up the pillars of it.
PSALM 75:3

606

Then shall thy light break forth as the morning, and thine
health shall spring forth speedily: and thy righteousness shall
go before thee; the glory of the LORD shall be thy reward.
ISAIAH 58:8

607

Keep therefore the words of this covenant, and do them,
that ye may prosper in all that ye do.
DEUTERONOMY 29:9

608

The spirit of a man will sustain his infirmity.
PROVERBS 18:14

609

Blessed are the meek: for they shall inherit the earth.
MATTHEW 5:5

610

*The righteous shall flourish like the palm tree: he shall
grow like a cedar in Lebanon. Those that be planted in the
house of the LORD shall flourish in the courts of our God.
They shall still bring forth fruit in old age;
they shall be fat and flourishing.*
PSALM 92:12–14

611

If ye know these things, happy are ye if ye do them.
JOHN 13:17

612

*So then faith cometh by hearing,
and hearing by the word of God.*
ROMANS 10:17

613

*The LORD is on my side; I will not fear:
what can man do unto me?*
PSALM 118:6

614

They that sow in tears shall reap in joy.
PSALM 126:5

615

But we all, with open face beholding as in a glass the glory
of the Lord, are changed into the same image from glory to
glory, even as by the Spirit of the Lord.
2 CORINTHIANS 3:18

616

I, even I, am he that comforteth you: who art thou,
that thou shouldest be afraid of a man that shall die,
and of the son of man which shall be made as grass.
ISAIAH 51:12

617

Of his own will begat he us with the word of truth,
that we should be a kind of firstfruits of his creatures.
JAMES 1:18

618

The LORD is my rock, and my fortress, and my deliverer;
my God, my strength, in whom I will trust; my buckler,
and the horn of my salvation, and my high tower.
PSALM 18:2

619

Commit thy way unto the LORD; trust also in him;
and he shall bring it to pass. And he shall bring
forth thy righteousness as the light, and thy
judgment as the noonday.
PSALM 37:5–6

620

*Wherefore we receiving a kingdom which cannot be
moved, let us have grace, whereby we may serve
God acceptably with reverence and godly fear.*
HEBREWS 12:28

621

*Ye are of God, little children, and have
overcome them: because greater is he that
is in you, than he that is in the world.*
1 JOHN 4:4

622

*For, brethren, ye have been called unto liberty;
only use not liberty for an occasion to the flesh,
but by love serve one another.*
GALATIANS 5:13

623

*And thou shalt do that which is right and good in the
sight of the Lord: that it may be well with thee,
and that thou mayest go in and possess the good
land which the LORD sware unto thy fathers.*
DEUTERONOMY 6:18

624

*And God shall wipe away all tears from their eyes;
and there shall be no more death, neither sorrow,
nor crying, neither shall there be any more pain:
for the former things are passed away.*
REVELATION 21:4

625

*Ah Lord God! behold, thou hast made the heaven
and the earth by thy great power and stretched
out arm, and there is nothing too hard for thee.*
JEREMIAH 32:17

626

*Be not wise in thine own eyes: fear the LORD,
and depart from evil. It shall be health
to thy navel, and marrow to thy bones.*
PROVERBS 3:7–8

627

*I will heal their backsliding, I will love them freely:
for mine anger is turned away from him.*
HOSEA 14:4

628

*Therefore my heart is glad, and my glory rejoiceth:
my flesh also shall rest in hope. For thou wilt not
leave my soul in hell; neither wilt thou suffer
thine Holy One to see corruption.*
PSALM 16:9–10

629

*Surely goodness and mercy shall follow me all the days of
my life: and I will dwell in the house of the LORD for ever.*
PSALM 23:6

630

*As for God, his way is perfect; the word of the LORD
is tried: he is a buckler to all them that trust in him.*
2 SAMUEL 22:31

631

And the LORD *shall help them, and deliver them:*
he shall deliver them from the wicked, and save them,
because they trust in him.
PSALM 37:40

632

Blessed are the pure in heart: for they shall see God.
MATTHEW 5:8

633

For we have not an high priest which cannot be touched
with the feeling of our infirmities; but was in all points
tempted like as we are, yet without sin. Let us therefore
come boldly unto the throne of grace, that we may obtain
mercy, and find grace to help in time of need.
HEBREWS 4:15–16

634

Heaven and earth shall pass away:
but my words shall not pass away.
LUKE 21:33

635

Likewise, I say unto you, there is joy in the presence
of the angels of God over one sinner that repenteth.
LUKE 15:10

636

They that hate thee shall be clothed with shame; and the
dwelling place of the wicked shall come to nought.
JOB 8:22

637

*Be not afraid of sudden fear, neither of the desolation of
the wicked, when it cometh. For the LORD shall be thy
confidence, and shall keep thy foot from being taken.*
PROVERBS 3:25–26

638

*Blessed are they that do his commandments,
that they may have right to the tree of life,
and may enter in through the gates into the city.*
REVELATION 22:14

639

*Who will render to every man according to his deeds: to
them who by patient continuance in well doing seek for
glory and honour and immortality, eternal life.*
ROMANS 2:6–7

640

*For I the LORD thy God will hold thy right hand,
saying unto thee, Fear not; I will help thee.*
ISAIAH 41:13

641

*They send forth their little ones like a flock,
and their children dance.*
JOB 21:11

642

*For the oppression of the poor, for the sighing of the needy,
now will I arise, saith the LORD; I will set him
in safety from him that puffeth at him.*
PSALM 12:5

643

But thou, when thou prayest, enter into thy closet,
and when thou hast shut thy door, pray to thy Father
which is in secret; and thy Father which seeth
in secret shall reward thee openly.

MATTHEW 6:6

644

For in the time of trouble he shall hide me in his pavilion:
in the secret of his tabernacle shall he hide me; he shall set
me up upon a rock. And now shall mine head be lifted up
above mine enemies round about me: therefore will I offer
in his tabernacle sacrifices of joy; I will sing, yea,
I will sing praises unto the LORD.

PSALM 27:5–6

645

See now that I, even I, am he, and there is no god with
me: I kill, and I make alive; I wound, and I heal:
neither is there any that can deliver out of my hand.

DEUTERONOMY 32:39

646

Are not five sparrows sold for two farthings, and not one
of them is forgotten before God? But even the very hairs
of your head are all numbered. Fear not therefore:
ye are of more value than many sparrows.

LUKE 12:6–7

647

But now being made free from sin, and become
servants to God, ye have your fruit unto
holiness, and the end everlasting life.

ROMANS 6:22

648

The hoary head is a crown of glory,
if it be found in the way of righteousness.
PROVERBS 16:31

649

The eyes of the LORD preserve knowledge, and he
overthroweth the words of the transgressor.
PROVERBS 22:12

650

Be not forgetful to entertain strangers: for thereby
some have entertained angels unawares.
HEBREWS 13:2

651

For there is hope of a tree, if it be cut down, that it will sprout
again, and that the tender branch thereof will not cease.
JOB 14:7

652

Though he fall, he shall not be utterly cast down:
for the LORD upholdeth him with his hand.
PSALM 37:24

653

Unto thee, O my strength, will I sing:
for God is my defence, and the God of my mercy.
PSALM 59:17

654

I will bless the LORD, who hath given me counsel:
my reins also instruct me in the night seasons.
PSALM 16:7

655

I exhort therefore, that, first of all, supplications, prayers, intercessions, and giving of thanks, be made for all men; for kings, and for all that are in authority; that we may lead a quiet and peaceable life in all godliness and honesty. For this is good and acceptable in the sight of God our Saviour; who will have all men to be saved, and to come unto the knowledge of the truth.

1 Timothy 2:1–4

656

For the eyes of the Lord run to and fro throughout the whole earth, to shew himself strong in the behalf of them whose heart is perfect toward him. Herein thou hast done foolishly: therefore from henceforth thou shalt have wars.

2 Chronicles 16:9

657

Be ye mindful always of his covenant; the word which he commanded to a thousand generations.

1 Chronicles 16:15

658

Yet the Lord will command his lovingkindness in the day time, and in the night his song shall be with me, and my prayer unto the God of my life.

Psalm 42:8

659

He raiseth up the poor out of the dust, and lifteth the needy out of the dunghill.

Psalm 113:7

660

And he arose, and rebuked the wind,
and said unto the sea, Peace, be still. And the
wind ceased, and there was a great calm.
MARK 4:39

661

For thou wilt light my candle:
the LORD my God will enlighten my darkness.
PSALM 18:28

662

But if the wicked will turn from all his sins that he hath
committed, and keep all my statutes, and do that which is
lawful and right, he shall surely live, he shall not die.
All his transgressions that he hath committed,
they shall not be mentioned unto him: in his
righteousness that he hath done he shall live.
EZEKIEL 18:21–22

663

Yea, though I walk through the valley of the shadow
of death, I will fear no evil: for thou art with me;
thy rod and thy staff they comfort me.
PSALM 23:4

664

Because of his strength will I wait upon thee: for God
is my defence. The God of my mercy shall prevent me:
God shall let me see my desire upon mine enemies.
PSALM 59:9–10

665

The righteous also shall hold on his way, and he that hath clean hands shall be stronger and stronger.

JOB 17:9

666

Why art thou cast down, O my soul? and why art thou disquieted within me? hope thou in God: for I shall yet praise him, who is the health of my countenance, and my God.

PSALM 42:11

667

He that walketh with wise men shall be wise: but a companion of fools shall be destroyed.

PROVERBS 13:20

668

The LORD taketh my part with them that help me: therefore shall I see my desire upon them that hate me.

PSALM 118:7

669

Thy word is true from the beginning: and every one of thy righteous judgments endureth for ever.

PSALM 119:160

670

Blessed are the merciful: for they shall obtain mercy.

MATTHEW 5:7

671

And he said unto them, Why are ye troubled? and why do thoughts arise in your hearts? Behold my hands and my feet, that it is I myself: handle me, and see; for a spirit hath not flesh and bones, as ye see me have.

LUKE 24:38–39

672

Therefore shall ye lay up these my words in your heart and in your soul, and bind them for a sign upon your hand, that they may be as frontlets between your eyes.

DEUTERONOMY 11:18

673

Jesus said unto him, If thou canst believe, all things are possible to him that believeth.

MARK 9:23

674

Thy dead men shall live, together with my dead body shall they arise. Awake and sing, ye that dwell in dust: for thy dew is as the dew of herbs, and the earth shall cast out the dead.

ISAIAH 26:19

675

With the ancient is wisdom; and in length of days understanding. With him is wisdom and strength, he hath counsel and understanding.

JOB 12:12–13

676

He delivereth me from mine enemies: yea, thou liftest me
up above those that rise up against me: thou hast
delivered me from the violent man.
PSALM 18:48

677

Yea, let none that wait on thee be ashamed: let them
be ashamed which transgress without cause.
PSALM 25:3

678

For the wages of sin is death; but the gift of God is
eternal life through Jesus Christ our Lord.
ROMANS 6:23

679

For since by man came death, by man came
also the resurrection of the dead.
1 CORINTHIANS 15:21

680

And hath put all things under his feet, and gave
him to be the head over all things to the church.
EPHESIANS 1:22

681

Lord, who shall abide in thy tabernacle? who shall dwell
in thy holy hill? He that walketh uprightly, and worketh
righteousness, and speaketh the truth in his heart.
PSALM 15:1–2

682

For I will be merciful to their unrighteousness, and their
sins and their iniquities will I remember no more.
HEBREWS 8:12

683

In this was manifested the love of God toward us,
because that God sent his only begotten Son into
the world, that we might live through him.
1 JOHN 4:9

684

This I say then, Walk in the Spirit,
and ye shall not fulfil the lust of the flesh.
GALATIANS 5:16

685

I know both how to be abased, and I know how to abound:
every where and in all things I am instructed both to be
full and to be hungry, both to abound and to suffer need.
I can do all things through Christ which strengtheneth me.
PHILIPPIANS 4:12–13

686

The voice of rejoicing and salvation is in the tabernacles of
the righteous: the right hand of the LORD doeth valiantly.
PSALM 118:15

687

Surely he scorneth the scorners:
but he giveth grace unto the lowly.
PROVERBS 3:34

688

But the path of the just is as the shining light,
that shineth more and more unto the perfect day.
PROVERBS 4:18

689

Keep thy heart with all diligence;
for out of it are the issues of life.
PROVERBS 4:23

690

The entrance of thy words giveth light;
it giveth understanding unto the simple.
PSALM 119:130

691

In famine he shall redeem thee from death:
and in war from the power of the sword.
JOB 5:20

692

Glory and honour are in his presence;
strength and gladness are in his place.
1 CHRONICLES 16:27

693

Our fathers trusted in thee: they trusted, and thou didst
deliver them. They cried unto thee, and were delivered:
they trusted in thee, and were not confounded.
PSALM 22:4–5

694

Which is come unto you, as it is in all the world;
and bringeth forth fruit, as it doth also in you, since the
day ye heard of it, and knew the grace of God in truth.
Colossians 1:6

695

Lead me in thy truth, and teach me: for thou art the
God of my salvation; on thee do I wait all the day.
Psalm 25:5

696

Who is a God like unto thee, that pardoneth iniquity, and
passeth by the transgression of the remnant of his heritage?
he retaineth not his anger for ever, because he delighteth in
mercy. He will turn again, he will have compassion upon
us; he will subdue our iniquities; and thou wilt cast all
their sins into the depths of the sea.
Micah 7:18–19

697

Let, I pray thee, thy merciful kindness be for my comfort,
according to thy word unto thy servant.
Psalm 119:76

698

Where no counsel is, the people fall:
but in the multitude of counsellors there is safety.
Proverbs 11:14

699

The Lord our God be with us, as he was with
our fathers: let him not leave us, nor forsake us.
1 Kings 8:57

700

And in every work that he began in the service of the house of God, and in the law, and in the commandments, to seek his God, he did it with all his heart, and prospered.

2 Chronicles 31:21

701

I am the Lord: that is my name: and my glory will I not give to another, neither my praise to graven images. Behold, the former things are come to pass, and new things do I declare: before they spring forth I tell you of them.

Isaiah 42:8–9

702

That they might set their hope in God, and not forget the works of God.

Psalm 78:7

703

Submit yourselves therefore to God. Resist the devil, and he will flee from you.

James 4:7

704

For then shalt thou have thy delight in the Almighty, and shalt lift up thy face unto God.

Job 22:26

705

For every one that asketh receiveth; and he that seeketh findeth; and to him that knocketh it shall be opened.

Matthew 7:8

706

The light of the eyes rejoiceth the heart:
and a good report maketh the bones fat.
PROVERBS 15:30

707

Behold, the heaven and the heaven of heavens is the
LORD's thy God, the earth also, with all that therein is.
DEUTERONOMY 10:14

708

For thus saith the Lord God, the Holy One of Israel;
In returning and rest shall ye be saved; in quietness and
in confidence shall be your strength: and ye would not.
ISAIAH 30:15

709

The LORD hath chastened me sore:
but he hath not given me over unto death.
PSALM 118:18

710

The LORD shall reign for ever, even thy God, O Zion,
unto all generations. Praise ye the LORD.
PSALM 146:10

711

Blessed is he that readeth, and they that hear the
words of this prophecy, and keep those things which
are written therein: for the time is at hand.
REVELATION 1:3

712

And we know that the Son of God is come, and hath given us an understanding, that we may know him that is true, and we are in him that is true, even in his Son Jesus Christ. This is the true God, and eternal life.

1 JOHN 5:20

713

The meek shall eat and be satisfied: they shall praise the LORD that seek him: your heart shall live for ever.

PSALM 22:26

714

And thou, Solomon my son, know thou the God of thy father, and serve him with a perfect heart and with a willing mind: for the LORD searcheth all hearts, and understandeth all the imaginations of the thoughts: if thou seek him, he will be found of thee; but if thou forsake him, he will cast thee off for ever.

1 CHRONICLES 28:9

715

And it came to pass in process of time, that the king of Egypt died: and the children of Israel sighed by reason of the bondage, and they cried, and their cry came up unto God by reason of the bondage. And God heard their groaning, and God remembered his covenant with Abraham, with Isaac, and with Jacob. And God looked upon the children of Israel, and God had respect unto them.

EXODUS 2:23–25

716

I have been young, and now am old; yet have I not seen
the righteous forsaken, nor his seed begging bread.
PSALM 37:25

717

Blessed are the peacemakers:
for they shall be called the children of God.
MATTHEW 5:9

718

Let no man deceive himself. If any man among you seemeth
to be wise in this world, let him become a fool, that he may be
wise. For the wisdom of this world is foolishness with God.
For it is written, He taketh the wise in their own craftiness.
1 CORINTHIANS 3:18–19

719

Wherefore take unto you the whole armour of God,
that ye may be able to withstand in the evil day,
and having done all, to stand.
EPHESIANS 6:13

720

For he hath not despised nor abhorred the affliction
of the afflicted; neither hath he hid his face from him;
but when he cried unto him, he heard.
PSALM 22:24

721

But I will deliver thee in that day, saith the Lord:
*and thou shalt not be given into the hand of the men
of whom thou art afraid. For I will surely deliver thee,
and thou shalt not fall by the sword, but thy life shall
be for a prey unto thee: because thou hast put thy
trust in me, saith the* Lord.

Jeremiah 39:17–18

722

For I the Lord *thy God will hold thy right hand,
saying unto thee, Fear not; I will help thee.*

Isaiah 41:13

723

*And of his fulness have all we received,
and grace for grace. For the law was given by Moses,
but grace and truth came by Jesus Christ.*

John 1:16–17

724

*He shall call upon me, and I will answer him: I will be
with him in trouble; I will deliver him, and honour him.*

Psalm 91:15

725

He is ever merciful, and lendeth; and his seed is blessed.

Psalm 37:26

726

*If we say that we have no sin, we deceive ourselves,
and the truth is not in us. If we confess our sins,
he is faithful and just to forgive us our sins,
and to cleanse us from all unrighteousness.*

1 John 1:8–9

727

And that from a child thou hast known the holy scriptures,
which are able to make thee wise unto salvation
through faith which is in Christ Jesus.

2 TIMOTHY 3:15

728

O that there were such an heart in them, that they would
fear me, and keep all my commandments always, that it
might be well with them, and with their children for ever!

DEUTERONOMY 5:29

729

Behold, happy is the man whom God correcteth: therefore
despise not thou the chastening of the Almighty: for he maketh
sore, and bindeth up: he woundeth, and his hands make whole.

JOB 5:17–18

730

Mark the perfect man, and behold the upright:
for the end of that man is peace.

PSALM 37:37

731

My covenant will I not break,
nor alter the thing that is gone out of my lips.

PSALM 89:34

732

The LORD is my shepherd; I shall not want. He maketh me
to lie down in green pastures: he leadeth me beside the still
waters. He restoreth my soul: he leadeth me in the paths
of righteousness for his name's sake.

PSALM 23:1–3

733

But now thus saith the LORD that created thee, O Jacob, and he that formed thee, O Israel, Fear not: for I have redeemed thee, I have called thee by thy name; thou art mine.

ISAIAH 43:1

734

Whoso eateth my flesh, and drinketh my blood, hath eternal life; and I will raise him up at the last day.

JOHN 6:54

735

Peace I leave with you, my peace I give unto you: not as the world giveth, give I unto you. Let not your heart be troubled, neither let it be afraid.

JOHN 14:27

736

There is therefore now no condemnation to them which are in Christ Jesus, who walk not after the flesh, but after the Spirit.

ROMANS 8:1

737

These things I have spoken unto you, that in me ye might have peace. In the world ye shall have tribulation: but be of good cheer; I have overcome the world.

JOHN 16:33

738

Am I a God at hand, saith the LORD, and not a God afar off? Can any hide himself in secret places that I shall not see him? saith the LORD. Do not I fill heaven and earth? saith the LORD.

JEREMIAH 23:23–24

739

For this is my blood of the new testament,
which is shed for many for the remission of sins.
MATTHEW 26:28

740

But the anointing which ye have received of him abideth in
you, and ye need not that any man teach you: but as the same
anointing teacheth you of all things, and is truth, and is no
lie, and even as it hath taught you, ye shall abide in him.
1 JOHN 2:27

741

I am come a light into the world, that whosoever
believeth on me should not abide in darkness.
JOHN 12:46

742

And he said, It is a light thing that thou shouldest
be my servant to raise up the tribes of Jacob, and to
restore the preserved of Israel: I will also give thee
for a light to the Gentiles, that thou mayest be
my salvation unto the end of the earth.
ISAIAH 49:6

743

If any of thine be driven out unto the outmost parts of
heaven, from thence will the LORD thy God gather thee,
and from thence will he fetch thee.
DEUTERONOMY 30:4

744

*The LORD is my light and my salvation; whom shall I fear?
the LORD is the strength of my life; of whom shall I be afraid?
When the wicked, even mine enemies and my foes, came upon
me to eat up my flesh, they stumbled and fell. Though an host
should encamp against me, my heart shall not fear: though
war should rise against me, in this will I be confident.*

PSALM 27:1–3

745

*If ye abide in me, and my words abide in you, ye shall
ask what ye will, and it shall be done unto you.*

JOHN 15:7

746

*And the Lord said, If ye had faith as a grain of mustard seed,
ye might say unto this sycamine tree, Be thou plucked up by the
root, and be thou planted in the sea; and it should obey you.*

LUKE 17:6

747

*And the peace of God, which passeth all understanding,
shall keep your hearts and minds through Christ Jesus.*

PHILIPPIANS 4:7

748

*And thine ears shall hear a word behind thee, saying,
This is the way, walk ye in it, when ye turn to the
right hand, and when ye turn to the left.*

ISAIAH 30:21

749

For the ways of man are before the eyes of the LORD,
and he pondereth all his goings.

PROVERBS 5:21

750

For the commandment is a lamp; and the law is light;
and reproofs of instruction are the way of life.

PROVERBS 6:23

751

But whoso looketh into the perfect law of liberty, and
continueth therein, he being not a forgetful hearer, but a
doer of the work, this man shall be blessed in his deed.

JAMES 1:25

752

For the grace of God that bringeth salvation hath appeared
to all men, teaching us that, denying ungodliness and
worldly lusts, we should live soberly, righteously, and godly,
in this present world.

TITUS 2:11–12

753

He that hath my commandments, and keepeth them, he it is
that loveth me: and he that loveth me shall be loved of my
Father, and I will love him, and will manifest myself to him.

JOHN 14:21

754

Children's children are the crown of old men;
and the glory of children are their fathers.

PROVERBS 17:6

755

*He hath made every thing beautiful in his time: also he hath
set the world in their heart, so that no man can find out the
work that God maketh from the beginning to the end.*

ECCLESIASTES 3:11

756

A sound heart is the life of the flesh.

PROVERBS 14:30

757

*Labour not for the meat which perisheth, but for that meat
which endureth unto everlasting life, which the Son of man
shall give unto you: for him hath God the Father sealed.*

JOHN 6:27

758

*And let us not be weary in well doing:
for in due season we shall reap, if we faint not.*

GALATIANS 6:9

759

*And as it is appointed unto men once to die, but after this
the judgment: so Christ was once offered to bear the sins of
many; and unto them that look for him shall he appear the
second time without sin unto salvation.*

HEBREWS 9:27–28

760

*He that cometh from above is above all: he that is of
the earth is earthly, and speaketh of the earth:
he that cometh from heaven is above all.*

JOHN 3:31

761

Depart from evil, and do good; and dwell for evermore.
For the LORD loveth judgment, and forsaketh not his
saints; they are preserved for ever: but the
seed of the wicked shall be cut off.
PSALM 37:27–28

762

And righteousness shall be the girdle of his loins,
and faithfulness the girdle of his reins.
ISAIAH 11:5

763

A merry heart doeth good like a medicine.
PROVERBS 17:22

764

He that tilleth his land shall have plenty of bread: but he
that followeth after vain persons shall have poverty enough.
PROVERBS 28:19

765

Arise therefore, and get thee down, and go with them,
doubting nothing: for I have sent them.
ACTS 10:20

766

But as it is written, Eye hath not seen, nor ear heard,
neither have entered into the heart of man, the things
which God hath prepared for them that love him.
1 CORINTHIANS 2:9

767

Forasmuch then as the children are partakers of flesh and blood, he also himself likewise took part of the same; that through death he might destroy him that had the power of death, that is, the devil; and deliver them who through fear of death were all their lifetime subject to bondage.

HEBREWS 2:14–15

768

For wisdom is better than rubies; and all the things that may be desired are not to be compared to it.

PROVERBS 8:11

769

Trouble and anguish have taken hold on me: yet thy commandments are my delights.

PSALM 119:143

770

He that believeth on me, as the scripture hath said, out of his belly shall flow rivers of living water.

JOHN 7:38

771

Thou shalt not be afraid of them: but shalt well remember what the LORD thy God did unto Pharaoh, and unto all Egypt.

DEUTERONOMY 7:18

772

Keep my commandments, and live; and my law as the apple of thine eye.

PROVERBS 7:2

773

Whosoever therefore shall break one of these least commandments, and shall teach men so, he shall be called the least in the kingdom of heaven: but whosoever shall do and teach them, the same shall be called great in the kingdom of heaven.

MATTHEW 5:19

774

Blessed is the man whose strength is in thee; in whose heart are the ways of them. Who passing through the valley of Baca make it a well; the rain also filleth the pools.

PSALM 84:5–6

775

I will be as the dew unto Israel: he shall grow as the lily, and cast forth his roots as Lebanon.

HOSEA 14:5

776

Give instruction to a wise man, and he will be yet wiser: teach a just man, and he will increase in learning.

PROVERBS 9:9

777

He becometh poor that dealeth with a slack hand: but the hand of the diligent maketh rich.

PROVERBS 10:4

778

And the light shineth in darkness; and the darkness comprehended it not.

JOHN 1:5

779

But thou shalt remember the LORD thy God: for it is he that giveth thee power to get wealth, that he may establish his covenant which he sware unto thy fathers, as it is this day.
DEUTERONOMY 8:18

780

If we believe not, yet he abideth faithful: he cannot deny himself.
2 TIMOTHY 2:13

781

And my people shall dwell in a peaceable habitation, and in sure dwellings, and in quiet resting places.
ISAIAH 32:18

782

Whom having not seen, ye love; in whom, though now ye see him not, yet believing, ye rejoice with joy unspeakable and full of glory: receiving the end of your faith, even the salvation of your souls.
1 PETER 1:8–9

783

And he sat down, and called the twelve, and saith unto them, If any man desire to be first, the same shall be last of all, and servant of all.
MARK 9:35

784

It is the spirit that quickeneth; the flesh profiteth nothing: the words that I speak unto you, they are spirit, and they are life.
JOHN 6:63

785

He that is slow to anger is better than the mighty;
and he that ruleth his spirit than he that taketh a city.
PROVERBS 16:32

786

A man's pride shall bring him low: but honour
shall uphold the humble in spirit.
PROVERBS 29:23

787

We are troubled on every side, yet not distressed; we are
perplexed, but not in despair; persecuted, but not
forsaken; cast down, but not destroyed.
2 CORINTHIANS 4:8–9

788

For ye had compassion of me in my bonds, and took joyfully
the spoiling of your goods, knowing in yourselves that ye
have in heaven a better and an enduring substance.
HEBREWS 10:34

789

I will hear what God the LORD will speak: for he
will speak peace unto his people, and to his saints:
but let them not turn again to folly.
PSALM 85:8

790

*And it shall come to pass, if ye shall hearken diligently unto my commandments which I command you this day, to love the L*ORD *your God, and to serve him with all your heart and with all your soul, that I will give you the rain of your land in his due season, the first rain and the latter rain, that thou mayest gather in thy corn, and thy wine, and thine oil. And I will send grass in thy fields for thy cattle, that thou mayest eat and be full.*

DEUTERONOMY 11:13–15

791

*Although the fig tree shall not blossom, neither shall fruit be in the vines; the labour of the olive shall fail, and the fields shall yield no meat; the flock shall be cut off from the fold, and there shall be no herd in the stalls: yet I will rejoice in the L*ORD*, I will joy in the God of my salvation.*

HABAKKUK 3:17–18

792

*He that hath pity upon the poor lendeth unto the L*ORD*; and that which he hath given will he pay him again.*

PROVERBS 19:17

793

Lift up your eyes on high, and behold who hath created these things, that bringeth out their host by number: he calleth them all by names by the greatness of his might, for that he is strong in power; not one faileth.

ISAIAH 40:26

794

Henceforth there is laid up for me a crown of righteousness,
which the Lord, the righteous judge, shall give me at
that day: and not to me only, but unto all them
also that love his appearing.

2 TIMOTHY 4:8

795

And the fruit of righteousness is sown
in peace of them that make peace.

JAMES 3:18

796

Better is an handful with quietness, than both the
hands full with travail and vexation of spirit.

ECCLESIASTES 4:6

797

The fear of the LORD tendeth to life: and he that hath it
shall abide satisfied; he shall not be visited with evil.

PROVERBS 19:23

798

He that giveth unto the poor shall not lack: but he that
hideth his eyes shall have many a curse.

PROVERBS 28:27

799

He that walketh righteously, and speaketh uprightly; he
that despiseth the gain of oppressions, that shaketh his hands
from holding of bribes, that stoppeth his ears from hearing of
blood, and shutteth his eyes from seeing evil; he shall dwell
on high: his place of defence shall be the munitions of rocks:
bread shall be given him; his waters shall be sure.

ISAIAH 33:15–16

800

Thou shalt make thy prayer unto him, and he shall hear thee, and thou shalt pay thy vows.

Job 22:27

801

Then will I sprinkle clean water upon you, and ye shall be clean: from all your filthiness, and from all your idols, will I cleanse you.

Ezekiel 36:25

802

Blessed are they which are persecuted for righteousness' sake: for theirs is the kingdom of heaven.

Matthew 5:10

803

And the Levite, (because he hath no part nor inheritance with thee,) and the stranger, and the fatherless, and the widow, which are within thy gates, shall come, and shall eat and be satisfied; that the Lord thy God may bless thee in all the work of thine hand which thou doest.

Deuteronomy 14:29

804

He that believeth on the Son hath everlasting life: and he that believeth not the Son shall not see life; but the wrath of God abideth on him.

John 3:36

805

Abide in me, and I in you. As the branch cannot bear fruit of itself, except it abide in the vine; no more can ye, except ye abide in me. I am the vine, ye are the branches: he that abideth in me, and I in him, the same bringeth forth much fruit: for without me ye can do nothing.

John 15:4–5

806

He that spared not his own Son, but delivered him up for us all, how shall he not with him also freely give us all things?

Romans 8:32

807

For as the rain cometh down, and the snow from heaven, and returneth not thither, but watereth the earth, and maketh it bring forth and bud, that it may give seed to the sower, and bread to the eater: so shall my word be that goeth forth out of my mouth: it shall not return unto me void, but it shall accomplish that which I please, and it shall prosper in the thing whereto I sent it.

Isaiah 55:10–11

808

The thoughts of the diligent tend only to plenteousness; but of every one that is hasty only to want.

Proverbs 21:5

809

When thou passest through the waters, I will be with thee; and through the rivers, they shall not overflow thee: when thou walkest through the fire, thou shalt not be burned; neither shall the flame kindle upon thee.

Isaiah 43:2

810

*The God of my rock; in him will I trust: he is my shield,
and the horn of my salvation, my high tower, and my
refuge, my saviour; thou savest me from violence.*

2 SAMUEL 22:3

811

*That I may cause those that love me to inherit substance;
and I will fill their treasures.*

PROVERBS 8:21

812

*O satisfy us early with thy mercy;
that we may rejoice and be glad all our days.*

PSALM 90:14

813

*Let your conversation be without covetousness; and be
content with such things as ye have: for he hath said,
I will never leave thee, nor forsake thee.*

HEBREWS 13:5

814

*Now our Lord Jesus Christ himself, and God, even our
Father, which hath loved us, and hath given us everlasting
consolation and good hope through grace, comfort your
hearts, and stablish you in every good word and work.*

2 THESSALONIANS 2:16–17

815

*I love them that love me; and those that seek me early shall
find me. Riches and honour are with me; yea, durable riches
and righteousness. My fruit is better than gold, yea,
than fine gold; and my revenue than choice silver.*

PROVERBS 8:17–19

816

And I will put my spirit within you, and cause you to walk in my statutes, and ye shall keep my judgments, and do them.
EZEKIEL 36:27

817

Say not thou, I will recompense evil; but wait on the LORD, and he shall save thee.
PROVERBS 20:22

818

He shall cover thee with his feathers, and under his wings shalt thou trust: his truth shall be thy shield and buckler.
PSALM 91:4

819

And this is the Father's will which hath sent me, that of all which he hath given me I should lose nothing, but should raise it up again at the last day. And this is the will of him that sent me, that every one which seeth the Son, and believeth on him, may have everlasting life: and I will raise him up at the last day.
JOHN 6:39–40

820

And, behold, I come quickly; and my reward is with me, to give every man according as his work shall be. I am Alpha and Omega, the beginning and the end, the first and the last.
REVELATION 22:12–13

821

Correct thy son, and he shall give thee rest; yea, he shall give delight unto thy soul.
PROVERBS 29:17

822

*Since thou wast precious in my sight, thou hast been
honourable, and I have loved thee: therefore will
I give men for thee, and people for thy life.*
ISAIAH 43:4

823

*And now, brethren, I commend you to God, and to the
word of his grace, which is able to build you up, and to give
you an inheritance among all them which are sanctified.*
ACTS 20:32

824

*And his mercy is on them that fear
him from generation to generation.*
LUKE 1:50

825

*And all these blessings shall come on thee, and overtake
thee, if thou shalt hearken unto the voice of the LORD thy
God. Blessed shalt thou be in the city, and blessed shalt
thou be in the field. Blessed shall be the fruit of thy body,
and the fruit of thy ground, and the fruit of thy cattle, the
increase of thy kine, and the flocks of thy sheep. Blessed shall
be thy basket and thy store. Blessed shalt thou be when thou
comest in, and blessed shalt thou be when thou goest out.*
DEUTERONOMY 28:2–6

826

*Let your light so shine before men, that they may see your
good works, and glorify your Father which is in heaven.*
MATTHEW 5:16

827

Fear none of those things which thou shalt suffer: behold,
the devil shall cast some of you into prison, that ye may
be tried; and ye shall have tribulation ten days: be thou
faithful unto death, and I will give thee a crown of life.
REVELATION 2:10

828

For whom the Lord loveth he chasteneth, and scourgeth
every son whom he receiveth. If ye endure chastening,
God dealeth with you as with sons; for what son is
he whom the father chasteneth not?
HEBREWS 12:6–7

829

By humility and the fear of the
LORD are riches, and honour, and life.
PROVERBS 22:4

830

That he would grant unto us, that we being delivered out
of the hand of our enemies might serve him without fear.
LUKE 1:74

831

For the kingdom of God is not meat and drink; but
righteousness, and peace, and joy in the Holy Ghost.
ROMANS 14:17

832

But the salvation of the righteous is of the LORD:
he is their strength in the time of trouble.
PSALM 37:39

833

*And when he was come into the house, the blind men came
to him: and Jesus saith unto them, Believe ye that I am able
to do this? They said unto him, Yea, Lord. Then touched he
their eyes, saying, According to your faith be it unto you.
And their eyes were opened; and Jesus straitly charged
them, saying, See that no man know it.*

MATTHEW 9:28–30

834

*For whatsoever is born of God overcometh the world: and
this is the victory that overcometh the world, even our faith.*

1 JOHN 5:4

835

*The meek also shall increase their joy in the LORD, and the
poor among men shall rejoice in the Holy One of Israel.*

ISAIAH 29:19

836

*And the LORD shall make thee the head, and not the
tail; and thou shalt be above only, and thou shalt not be
beneath; if that thou hearken unto the commandments
of the Lord thy God, which I command thee
this day, to observe and to do them.*

DEUTERONOMY 28:13

837

*Have not I commanded thee? Be strong and of a good
courage; be not afraid, neither be thou dismayed: for the
LORD thy God is with thee whithersoever thou goest.*

JOSHUA 1:9

838

Pleasant words are as an honeycomb,
sweet to the soul, and health to the bones.
PROVERBS 16:24

839

The wicked plotteth against the just, and gnasheth
upon him with his teeth. The LORD shall laugh
at him: for he seeth that his day is coming.
PSALM 37:12–13

840

And whatsoever ye shall ask in my name, that will I do,
that the Father may be glorified in the Son. If ye
shall ask any thing in my name, I will do it.
JOHN 14:13–14

841

And shall not God avenge his own elect, which cry day
and night unto him, though he bear long with them?
LUKE 18:7

842

For in thee, O LORD, do I hope:
thou wilt hear, O Lord my God.
PSALM 38:15

843

While we look not at the things which are seen, but at the
things which are not seen: for the things which are seen are
temporal; but the things which are not seen are eternal.
2 CORINTHIANS 4:18

844

Even the youths shall faint and be weary, and the young
men shall utterly fall: but they that wait upon the LORD
shall renew their strength; they shall mount up with
wings as eagles; they shall run, and not be weary;
and they shall walk, and not faint.
ISAIAH 40:30–31

845

Call unto me, and I will answer thee, and show thee
great and mighty things, which thou knowest not.
JEREMIAH 33:3

846

All scripture is given by inspiration of God, and is
profitable for doctrine, for reproof, for correction, for
instruction in righteousness: that the man of God may
be perfect, thoroughly furnished unto all good works.
2 TIMOTHY 3:16–17

847

Behold, we count them happy which endure. Ye have heard
of the patience of Job, and have seen the end of the Lord;
that the Lord is very pitiful, and of tender mercy.
JAMES 5:11

848

When a man's ways please the LORD, he maketh
even his enemies to be at peace with him.
PROVERBS 16:7

849

We have also a more sure word of prophecy; whereunto
ye do well that ye take heed, as unto a light that
shineth in a dark place, until the day dawn,
and the day star arise in your hearts.

2 PETER 1:19

850

And as Moses lifted up the serpent in the wilderness,
even so must the Son of man be lifted up: that whosoever
believeth in him should not perish, but have eternal life.

JOHN 3:14–15

851

For he hath made him to be sin for us, who knew no sin;
that we might be made the righteousness of God in him.

2 CORINTHIANS 5:21

852

He that dwelleth in the secret place of the
most High shall abide under the shadow of
the Almighty. I will say of the LORD, He is my
refuge and my fortress: my God; in him will I trust.

PSALM 91:1–2

853

For a just man falleth seven times, and riseth up again:
but the wicked shall fall into mischief.

PROVERBS 24:16

854

*Wherefore gird up the loins of your mind, be sober,
and hope to the end for the grace that is to be brought
unto you at the revelation of Jesus Christ.*

1 PETER 1:13

855

*For every creature of God is good, and nothing to
be refused, if it be received with thanksgiving.*

1 TIMOTHY 4:4

856

*Behold, all they that were incensed against thee shall
be ashamed and confounded: they shall be as nothing;
and they that strive with thee shall perish. Thou shalt
seek them, and shalt not find them, even them that
contended with thee: they that war against thee
shall be as nothing, and as a thing of nought.*

ISAIAH 41:11–12

857

*Train up a child in the way he should go:
and when he is old, he will not depart from it.*

PROVERBS 22:6

858

*For thus saith the LORD, That after seventy years be
accomplished at Babylon I will visit you, and perform
my good word toward you, in causing you to return to
this place. For I know the thoughts that I think toward
you, saith the LORD, thoughts of peace, and not
of evil, to give you an expected end.*

JEREMIAH 29:10–11

859

Cast thy bread upon the waters:
for thou shalt find it after many days.
ECCLESIASTES 11:1

860

And thou shalt return and obey the voice of the LORD,
and do all his commandments which I command thee
this day. And the LORD thy God will make thee plenteous
in every work of thine hand, in the fruit of thy body,
and in the fruit of thy cattle, and in the fruit of thy
land, for good: for the LORD will again rejoice over
thee for good, as he rejoiced over thy fathers.
DEUTERONOMY 30:8–9

861

And this is the record, that God hath given
to us eternal life, and this life is in his Son.
1 JOHN 5:11

862

And he went out to meet Asa, and said unto him, Hear ye
me, Asa, and all Judah and Benjamin; The LORD is with
you, while ye be with him; and if ye seek him, he will be
found of you; but if ye forsake him, he will forsake you.
2 CHRONICLES 15:2

863

Behold my servant, whom I uphold; mine elect, in whom my soul delighteth; I have put my spirit upon him: he shall bring forth judgment to the Gentiles. He shall not cry, nor lift up, nor cause his voice to be heard in the street. A bruised reed shall he not break, and the smoking flax shall he not quench: he shall bring forth judgment unto truth. He shall not fail nor be discouraged, till he have set judgment in the earth: and the isles shall wait for his law.

Isaiah 42:1–4

864

The fear of man bringeth a snare: but whoso putteth his trust in the Lord shall be safe.

Proverbs 29:25

865

Thou shalt also decree a thing, and it shall be established unto thee: and the light shall shine upon thy ways.

Job 22:28

866

These things have I written unto you that believe on the name of the Son of God; that ye may know that ye have eternal life, and that ye may believe on the name of the Son of God.

1 John 5:13

867

For God sent not his Son into the world to condemn the world; but that the world through him might be saved.

John 3:17

868

For he shall deliver the needy when he crieth; the poor also,
and him that hath no helper. He shall spare the poor
and needy, and shall save the souls of the needy.
PSALM 72:12–13

869

The LORD knoweth the days of the upright:
and their inheritance shall be for ever.
PSALM 37:18

870

Then shalt thou call, and the LORD shall answer;
thou shalt cry, and he shall say, Here I am. If thou
take away from the midst of thee the yoke, the putting
forth of the finger, and speaking vanity.
ISAIAH 58:9

871

And Moses said unto the people, Fear ye not, stand still,
and see the salvation of the LORD, which he will shew to
you to day: for the Egyptians whom ye have seen to day,
ye shall see them again no more for ever. The LORD
shall fight for you, and ye shall hold your peace.
EXODUS 14:13–14

872

Thou art my hiding place and my shield:
I hope in thy word.
PSALM 119:114

873

Then spake Jesus again unto them, saying, I am the light of the world: he that followeth me shall not walk in darkness, but shall have the light of life.

John 8:12

874

For whosoever shall give you a cup of water to drink in my name, because ye belong to Christ, verily I say unto you, he shall not lose his reward.

Mark 9:41

875

And David said to Solomon his son, Be strong and of good courage, and do it: fear not, nor be dismayed: for the Lord God, even my God, will be with thee; he will not fail thee, nor forsake thee, until thou hast finished all the work for the service of the house of the Lord.

1 Chronicles 28:20

876

For they verily for a few days chastened us after their own pleasure; but he for our profit, that we might be partakers of his holiness. Now no chastening for the present seemeth to be joyous, but grievous: nevertheless afterward it yieldeth the peaceable fruit of righteousness unto them which are exercised thereby.

Hebrews 12:10–11

877

My doctrine shall drop as the rain, my speech shall distil as the dew, as the small rain upon the tender herb, and as the showers upon the grass.

Deuteronomy 32:2

878

Blessed is the people that know the joyful sound:
they shall walk, O LORD, in the light of thy countenance.
In thy name shall they rejoice all the day: and in thy
righteousness shall they be exalted.

PSALM 89:15–16

879

Hast thou faith? have it to thyself before God.
Happy is he that condemneth not himself
in that thing which he alloweth.

ROMANS 14:22

880

If thine enemy be hungry, give him bread to eat; and if
he be thirsty, give him water to drink: for thou shalt heap
coals of fire upon his head, and the LORD shall reward thee.

PROVERBS 25:21–22

881

And if thou draw out thy soul to the hungry, and satisfy
the afflicted soul; then shall thy light rise in obscurity,
and thy darkness be as the noon day.

ISAIAH 58:10

882

(For we walk by faith, not by sight:) we are confident,
I say, and willing rather to be absent from the body,
and to be present with the Lord.

2 CORINTHIANS 5:7–8

883

I have many things to say and to judge of you:
but he that sent me is true; and I speak to the
world those things which I have heard of him.
JOHN 8:26

884

He delivereth the poor in his affliction,
and openeth their ears in oppression.
JOB 36:15

885

And he said unto them, Verily I say unto you, There is
no man that hath left house, or parents, or brethren,
or wife, or children, for the kingdom of God's sake,
who shall not receive manifold more in this present
time, and in the world to come life everlasting.
LUKE 18:29–30

886

For he that soweth to his flesh shall of the flesh
reap corruption; but he that soweth to the Spirit
shall of the Spirit reap life everlasting.
GALATIANS 6:8

887

And refused to obey, neither were mindful of thy wonders
that thou didst among them; but hardened their necks,
and in their rebellion appointed a captain to return to their
bondage: but thou art a God ready to pardon, gracious
and merciful, slow to anger, and of great kindness,
and forsookest them not.
NEHEMIAH 9:17

888

I waited patiently for the LORD; and he inclined unto me, and heard my cry. He brought me up also out of an horrible pit, out of the miry clay, and set my feet upon a rock, and established my goings. And he hath put a new song in my mouth, even praise unto our God: many shall see it, and fear, and shall trust in the LORD.

PSALM 40:1–3

889

Thy word is a lamp unto my feet, and a light unto my path.

PSALM 119:105

890

Blessed are ye, when men shall revile you, and persecute you, and shall say all manner of evil against you falsely, for my sake. Rejoice, and be exceeding glad: for great is your reward in heaven: for so persecuted they the prophets which were before you.

MATTHEW 5:11–12

891

But the LORD your God ye shall fear; and he shall deliver you out of the hand of all your enemies.

2 KINGS 17:39

892

Now therefore hearken unto me, O ye children: for blessed are they that keep my ways. Hear instruction, and be wise, and refuse it not.

PROVERBS 8:32–33

893

*To appoint unto them that mourn in Zion, to give unto
them beauty for ashes, the oil of joy for mourning,
the garment of praise for the spirit of heaviness; that they
might be called trees of righteousness, the planting
of the LORD, that he might be glorified.*

ISAIAH 61:3

894

*Be afflicted, and mourn, and weep: let your laughter be
turned to mourning, and your joy to heaviness. Humble
yourselves in the sight of the Lord, and he shall lift you up.*

JAMES 4:9–10

895

*And this is the confidence that we have in him, that, if we
ask any thing according to his will, he heareth us: and if
we know that he hear us, whatsoever we ask, we know
that we have the petitions that we desired of him.*

1 JOHN 5:14–15

896

*Where there is no vision, the people perish:
but he that keepeth the law, happy is he.*

PROVERBS 29:18

897

*Jesus said unto her, I am the resurrection, and the life:
he that believeth in me, though he were dead, yet shall
he live: and whosoever liveth and believeth in
me shall never die. Believest thou this?*

JOHN 11:25–26

898

*Nevertheless God, that comforteth those that are
cast down, comforted us by the coming of Titus.*
2 Corinthians 7:6

899

*Even the mystery which hath been hid from ages and
from generations, but now is made manifest to his saints:
to whom God would make known what is the riches of
the glory of this mystery among the Gentiles; which is
Christ in you, the hope of glory.*
Colossians 1:26–27

900

*When men are cast down, then thou shalt say, There is
lifting up; and he shall save the humble person.*
Job 22:29

901

*If his children forsake my law, and walk not in my judgments;
if they break my statutes, and keep not my commandments;
then will I visit their transgression with the rod, and their
iniquity with stripes. Nevertheless my lovingkindness will I
not utterly take from him, nor suffer my faithfulness to fail.*
Psalm 89:30–33

902

*Before I formed thee in the belly I knew thee; and before
thou camest forth out of the womb I sanctified thee.*
Jeremiah 1:5

903

*There is that scattereth, and yet increaseth; and there
is that withholdeth more than is meet, but it tendeth
to poverty. The liberal soul shall be made fat: and he
that watereth shall be watered also himself.*

PROVERBS 11:24–25

904

*And the prayer of faith shall save the sick,
and the Lord shall raise him up; and if he have
committed sins, they shall be forgiven him.*

JAMES 5:15

905

*For we brought nothing into this world, and it is
certain we can carry nothing out. And having
food and raiment let us be therewith content.*

1 TIMOTHY 6:7–8

906

*As for me, this is my covenant with them, saith the LORD;
My spirit that is upon thee, and my words which I have
put in thy mouth, shall not depart out of thy mouth, nor
out of the mouth of thy seed, nor out of the mouth of thy
seed's seed, saith the LORD, from henceforth and for ever.*

ISAIAH 59:21

907

*The LORD is nigh unto all them that call upon him,
to all that call upon him in truth.*

PSALM 145:18

908

Be still, and know that I am God: I will be exalted
among the heathen, I will be exalted in the earth.
Psalm 46:10

909

Thine, O Lord is the greatness, and the power, and the
glory, and the victory, and the majesty: for all that is in the
heaven and in the earth is thine; thine is the kingdom,
O Lord, and thou art exalted as head above all. Both
riches and honour come of thee, and thou reignest over all;
and in thine hand is power and might; and in thine hand
it is to make great, and to give strength unto all.
1 Chronicles 29:11–12

910

But I say unto you, Love your enemies, bless them that
curse you, do good to them that hate you, and pray for them
which despitefully use you, and persecute you; that ye may
be the children of your Father which is in heaven: for he
maketh his sun to rise on the evil and on the good, and
sendeth rain on the just and on the unjust.
Matthew 5:44–45

911

Through the tender mercy of our God; whereby the
dayspring from on high hath visited us, to give light to
them that sit in darkness and in the shadow of death,
to guide our feet into the way of peace.
Luke 1:78–79

912

Verily I say unto you, Wheresoever this gospel shall be preached throughout the whole world, this also that she hath done shall be spoken of for a memorial of her.

MARK 14:9

913

And his inward affection is more abundant toward you, whilst he remembereth the obedience of you all, how with fear and trembling ye received him.

2 CORINTHIANS 7:15

914

For our conversation is in heaven; from whence also we look for the Saviour, the Lord Jesus Christ: who shall change our vile body, that it may be fashioned like unto his glorious body, according to the working whereby he is able even to subdue all things unto himself.

PHILIPPIANS 3:20–21

915

But the LORD said unto Samuel, Look not on his countenance, or on the height of his stature; because I have refused him: for the LORD seeth not as man seeth; for man looketh on the outward appearance, but the LORD looketh on the heart.

1 SAMUEL 16:7

916

Blessed is he that considereth the poor: the LORD will deliver him in time of trouble. The LORD will preserve him, and keep him alive; and he shall be blessed upon the earth: and thou wilt not deliver him unto the will of his enemies.

PSALM 41:1–2

917

*Every man also to whom God hath given riches and wealth,
and hath given him power to eat thereof, and to take his
portion, and to rejoice in his labour; this is the gift of God.*
ECCLESIASTES 5:19

918

*For every one shall be salted with fire,
and every sacrifice shall be salted with salt.*
MARK 9:49

919

*In my Father's house are many mansions: if it were not so, I
would have told you. I go to prepare a place for you. And if I
go and prepare a place for you, I will come again, and receive
you unto myself; that where I am, there ye may be also.*
JOHN 14:2–3

920

*He that trusteth in his own heart is a fool:
but whoso walketh wisely, he shall be delivered.*
PROVERBS 28:26

921

*For I will pour water upon him that is thirsty, and floods
upon the dry ground: I will pour my spirit upon thy seed,
and my blessing upon thine offspring.*
ISAIAH 44:3

922

*For as a young man marrieth a virgin, so shall thy sons
marry thee: and as the bridegroom rejoiceth over
the bride, so shall thy God rejoice over thee.*
ISAIAH 62:5

923

And said unto them, Whosoever shall receive this child in
my name receiveth me: and whosoever shall receive me
receiveth him that sent me: for he that is least
among you all, the same shall be great.

LUKE 9:48

924

For I will not trust in my bow, neither shall my sword
save me. But thou hast saved us from our enemies,
and hast put them to shame that hated us.

PSALM 44:6–7

925

Jesus answered and said unto him, If a man love me,
he will keep my words: and my Father will love him, and
we will come unto him, and make our abode with him.

JOHN 14:23

926

But when Jesus saw it, he was much displeased, and said unto
them, Suffer the little children to come unto me, and forbid
them not: for of such is the kingdom of God. Verily I say unto
you, Whosoever shall not receive the kingdom of God as a little
child, he shall not enter therein. And he took them up in his
arms, put his hands upon them, and blessed them.

MARK 10:14–16

927

For my name's sake will I defer mine anger, and for my
praise will I refrain for thee, that I cut thee not off.

ISAIAH 48:9

928

*That they do good, that they be rich in good works, ready to
distribute, willing to communicate; laying up in store for
themselves a good foundation against the time to come,
that they may lay hold on eternal life.*

1 TIMOTHY 6:18–19

929

*And I heard a voice from heaven saying unto me,
Write, Blessed are the dead which die in the Lord from
henceforth: Yea, saith the Spirit, that they may rest from
their labours; and their works do follow them.*

REVELATION 14:13

930

*The sleep of a labouring man is sweet, whether he
eat little or much: but the abundance of the
rich will not suffer him to sleep.*

ECCLESIASTES 5:12

931

*If they obey and serve him, they shall spend their
days in prosperity, and their years in pleasures.*

JOB 36:11

932

*Declaring the end from the beginning, and from ancient
times the things that are not yet done, saying, My counsel
shall stand, and I will do all my pleasure.*

ISAIAH 46:10

933

He that hath a bountiful eye shall be blessed;
for he giveth of his bread to the poor.

PROVERBS 22:9

934

Remember the word unto thy servant, upon which thou
hast caused me to hope. This is my comfort in my affliction:
for thy word hath quickened me.

PSALM 119:49–50

935

And in that day ye shall ask me nothing. Verily, verily,
I say unto you, Whatsoever ye shall ask the Father in my
name, he will give it you. Hitherto have ye asked nothing in
my name: ask, and ye shall receive, that your joy may be full.

JOHN 16:23–24

936

Now unto him that is able to do exceeding abundantly
above all that we ask or think, according to the power that
worketh in us, unto him be glory in the church by Christ
Jesus throughout all ages, world without end.

EPHESIANS 3:20–21

937

Is not this laid up in store with me, and sealed up among
my treasures? To me belongeth vengeance and recompence;
their foot shall slide in due time: for the day of their
calamity is at hand, and the things that shall
come upon them make haste.

DEUTERONOMY 32:34–35

938

And even to your old age I am he; and even to hoar hairs will I carry you: I have made, and I will bear; even I will carry, and will deliver you.

ISAIAH 46:4

939

And there shall be no night there; and they need no candle, neither light of the sun; for the Lord God giveth them light: and they shall reign for ever and ever.

REVELATION 22:5

940

Every man according as he purposeth in his heart, so let him give; not grudgingly, or of necessity: for God loveth a cheerful giver.

2 CORINTHIANS 9:7

941

But the fruit of the Spirit is love, joy, peace, longsuffering, gentleness, goodness, faith, meekness, temperance: against such there is no law.

GALATIANS 5:22–23

942

I beseech you therefore, brethren, by the mercies of God, that ye present your bodies a living sacrifice, holy, acceptable unto God, which is your reasonable service. And be not conformed to this world: but be ye transformed by the renewing of your mind, that ye may prove what is that good, and acceptable, and perfect, will of God.

ROMANS 12:1–2

943

Through wisdom is an house builded; and by understanding
it is established: and by knowledge shall the chambers be
filled with all precious and pleasant riches.

PROVERBS 24:3–4

944

For ever, O LORD, thy word is settled in heaven.
Thy faithfulness is unto all generations: thou hast
established the earth, and it abideth.

PSALM 119:89–90

945

And God is able to make all grace abound toward you;
that ye, always having all sufficiency in all things,
may abound to every good work.

2 CORINTHIANS 9:8

946

Therefore are they before the throne of God, and serve him
day and night in his temple: and he that sitteth on the throne
shall dwell among them. They shall hunger no more, neither
thirst any more; neither shall the sun light on them, nor
any heat. For the Lamb which is in the midst of the throne
shall feed them, and shall lead them unto living fountains of
waters: and God shall wipe away all tears from their eyes.

REVELATION 7:15–17

947

Set your affection on things above, not on things on the earth.
For ye are dead, and your life is hid with Christ in God.

COLOSSIANS 3:2–3

948

I, even I, am he that blotteth out thy transgressions for mine own sake, and will not remember thy sins.

ISAIAH 43:25

949

Then said Jesus unto his disciples, If any man will come after me, let him deny himself, and take up his cross, and follow me. For whosoever will save his life shall lose it: and whosoever will lose his life for my sake shall find it.

MATTHEW 16:24–25

950

Being born again, not of corruptible seed, but of incorruptible, by the word of God, which liveth and abideth for ever.

1 PETER 1:23

951

If ye be reproached for the name of Christ, happy are ye; for the spirit of glory and of God resteth upon you: on their part he is evil spoken of, but on your part he is glorified.

1 PETER 4:14

952

And he said unto me, My grace is sufficient for thee: for my strength is made perfect in weakness. Most gladly therefore will I rather glory in my infirmities, that the power of Christ may rest upon me.

2 CORINTHIANS 12:9

953

Fret not thyself because of evil men, neither be thou envious
at the wicked: for there shall be no reward to the evil man;
the candle of the wicked shall be put out.

PROVERBS 24:19–20

954

I know that there is no good in them, but for a man
to rejoice, and to do good in his life. And also that
every man should eat and drink, and enjoy the
good of all his labour, it is the gift of God.

ECCLESIASTES 3:12–13

955

And I will pray the Father, and he shall give you another
Comforter, that he may abide with you for ever; even the
Spirit of truth; whom the world cannot receive, because it
seeth him not, neither knoweth him: but ye know him;
for he dwelleth with you, and shall be in you.

JOHN 14:16–17

956

With good will doing service, as to the Lord, and not to men:
knowing that whatsoever good thing any man doeth, the
same shall he receive of the Lord, whether he be bond or free.

EPHESIANS 6:7–8

957

The LORD lifteth up the meek:
he casteth the wicked down to the ground.

PSALM 147:6

958

The LORD preserveth all them that love him:
but all the wicked will he destroy.

PSALM 145:20

959

But God, who is rich in mercy, for his great love wherewith
he loved us, even when we were dead in sins, hath quickened
us together with Christ, (by grace ye are saved;) and hath
raised us up together, and made us sit together in heavenly
places in Christ Jesus: that in the ages to come he might
shew the exceeding riches of his grace in his kindness
toward us through Christ Jesus.

EPHESIANS 2:4–7

960

Sing, O heavens; and be joyful, O earth; and break forth
into singing, O mountains: for the LORD hath comforted
his people, and will have mercy upon his afflicted.

ISAIAH 49:13

961

For verily I say unto you, That whosoever shall say unto
this mountain, Be thou removed, and be thou cast into
the sea; and shall not doubt in his heart, but shall believe
that those things which he saith shall come to pass;
he shall have whatsoever he saith.

MARK 11:23

962

The Lord will perfect that which concerneth me:
thy mercy, O Lord, endureth for ever:
forsake not the works of thine own hands.
Psalm 138:8

963

The Lord is far from the wicked:
but he heareth the prayer of the righteous.
Proverbs 15:29

964

And the afflicted people thou wilt save: but thine eyes are
upon the haughty, that thou mayest bring them down.
2 Samuel 22:28

965

For the word of the Lord is right;
and all his works are done in truth.
Psalm 33:4

966

Blessed are they that keep his testimonies, and that
seek him with the whole heart. They also do
no iniquity: they walk in his ways.
Psalm 119:2–3

967

*For this cause shall a man leave his father and mother,
and cleave to his wife; and they twain shall be one flesh:
so then they are no more twain, but one flesh. What
therefore God hath joined together, let not man put asunder.*

MARK 10:7–9

968

*A seed shall serve him; it shall be accounted
to the Lord for a generation.*

PSALM 22:30

969

*But now, O LORD, thou art our father; we are the clay,
and thou our potter; and we all are the work of thy hand.*

ISAIAH 64:8

970

*And he said unto his disciples, Therefore I say unto you,
Take no thought for your life, what ye shall eat; neither for
the body, what ye shall put on. The life is more than meat,
and the body is more than raiment.*

LUKE 12:22–23

971

*Now the God of hope fill you with all joy and peace
in believing, that ye may abound in hope,
through the power of the Holy Ghost.*
ROMANS 15:13

972

*For now we see through a glass, darkly; but then face
to face: now I know in part; but then shall
I know even as also I am known.*
1 CORINTHIANS 13:12

973

*Thou hast dealt well with thy servant,
O LORD, according unto thy word.*
PSALM 119:65

974

*But speaking the truth in love, may grow up into him in
all things, which is the head, even Christ: from whom the
whole body fitly joined together and compacted by that
which every joint supplieth, according to the effectual
working in the measure of every part, maketh increase
of the body unto the edifying of itself in love.*
EPHESIANS 4:15–16

975

That he may incline our hearts unto him, to walk in all his ways, and to keep his commandments, and his statutes, and his judgments, which he commanded our fathers. And let these my words, wherewith I have made supplication before the LORD, be nigh unto the LORD our God day and night, that he maintain the cause of his servant, and the cause of his people Israel at all times, as the matter shall require.

1 KINGS 8:58–59

976

For by thee I have run through a troop;
and by my God have I leaped over a wall.

PSALM 18:29

977

For all flesh is as grass, and all the glory of man as the flower of grass. The grass withereth, and the flower thereof falleth away: but the word of the Lord endureth for ever. And this is the word which by the gospel is preached unto you.

1 PETER 1:24–25

978

For though he was crucified through weakness, yet he liveth by the power of God. For we also are weak in him, but we shall live with him by the power of God toward you.

2 CORINTHIANS 13:4

979

*But they which shall be accounted worthy to obtain that
world, and the resurrection from the dead, neither marry,
nor are given in marriage: neither can they die any more:
for they are equal unto the angels; and are the children of
God, being the children of the resurrection.*

LUKE 20:35–36

980

*Good and upright is the LORD:
therefore will he teach sinners in the way.*

PSALM 25:8

981

*And when ye stand praying, forgive, if ye have ought
against any: that your Father also which is in
heaven may forgive you your trespasses.*

MARK 11:25

982

*Come unto me, all ye that labour and are heavy laden,
and I will give you rest. Take my yoke upon you,
and learn of me; for I am meek and lowly in heart:
and ye shall find rest unto your souls.*

MATTHEW 11:28–29

983

A man's heart deviseth his way:
but the LORD directeth his steps.

PROVERBS 16:9

984

Calling a ravenous bird from the east, the man that executeth
my counsel from a far country: yea, I have spoken it, I will also
bring it to pass; I have purposed it, I will also do it.

ISAIAH 46:11

985

The words of the LORD are pure words: as silver tried
in a furnace of earth, purified seven times.

PSALM 12:6

986

But the Comforter, which is the Holy Ghost, whom the
Father will send in my name, he shall teach you all
things, and bring all things to your remembrance,
whatsoever I have said unto you.

JOHN 14:26

987

For we are saved by hope: but hope that is seen is not hope: for
what a man seeth, why doth he yet hope for? But if we hope
for that we see not, then do we with patience wait for it.

ROMANS 8:24–25

988

Finally, brethren, farewell. Be perfect, be of good comfort, be of one mind, live in peace; and the God of love and peace shall be with you.

2 Corinthians 13:11

989

And, behold, this day I am going the way of all the earth: and ye know in all your hearts and in all your souls, that not one thing hath failed of all the good things which the Lord your God spake concerning you; all are come to pass unto you, and not one thing hath failed thereof.

Joshua 23:14

990

Surely he hath borne our griefs, and carried our sorrows: yet we did esteem him stricken, smitten of God, and afflicted.

Isaiah 53:4

991

Whether Paul, or Apollos, or Cephas, or the world, or life, or death, or things present, or things to come; all are your's; and ye are Christ's; and Christ is God's.

1 Corinthians 3:22–23

992

Therefore if thine enemy hunger, feed him; if he thirst, give him drink: for in so doing thou shalt heap coals of fire on his head. Be not overcome of evil, but overcome evil with good.

Romans 12:20–21

993

Therefore my people shall know my name:
therefore they shall know in that day that
I am he that doth speak: behold, it is I.
Isaiah 52:6

994

And ye shall be hated of all men for my name's sake: but he
that shall endure unto the end, the same shall be saved.
Mark 13:13

995

Therefore, my beloved brethren, be ye stedfast, unmoveable,
always abounding in the work of the Lord, forasmuch as
ye know that your labour is not in vain in the Lord.
1 Corinthians 15:58

996

And they that know thy name will put their trust in thee:
for thou, Lord, hast not forsaken them that seek thee.
Psalm 9:10

997

And they shall build houses, and inhabit them; and they shall
plant vineyards, and eat the fruit of them. They shall not
build, and another inhabit; they shall not plant, and another
eat: for as the days of a tree are the days of my people, and
mine elect shall long enjoy the work of their hands.
Isaiah 65:21–22

998

Who his own self bare our sins in his own body on
the tree, that we, being dead to sins, should live unto
righteousness: by whose stripes ye were healed.

1 Peter 2:24

999

And if Christ be in you, the body is dead because of sin;
but the Spirit is life because of righteousness.

Romans 8:10

1,000

And when I saw him, I fell at his feet as dead. And he
laid his right hand upon me, saying unto me,
Fear not; I am the first and the last. . .

Revelation 1:17

1,001

Now unto him that is able to keep you from falling, and
to present you faultless before the presence of his glory with
exceeding joy, to the only wise God our Saviour, be glory and
majesty, dominion and power, both now and ever. Amen.

Jude 24–25

LOOKING FOR MORE ENCOURAGEMENT FOR YOUR HEART?

Worry Less, Pray More

This purposeful devotional guide features 180 readings and prayers designed to help alleviate your worries as you learn to live in the peace of the Almighty God, who offers calm for your anxiety-filled soul.

Paperback / 978-1-68322-861-5 / $4.99

Too Blessed to be Stressed: 3-Minute Devotions for Women

You'll find the spiritual pick-me-up you need in *Too Blessed to Be Stressed: 3-Minute Devotions for Women*. 180 uplifting readings from bestselling author Debora M. Coty pack a powerful dose of inspiration, encouragement, humor, and faith into just-right-sized readings for your busy schedule.

Paperback / 978-1-63409-569-3 / $4.99